BOB SCHIEFFER'S
AMERICA

ALSO BY BOB SCHIEFFER

BOOKS

*Face the Nation: My Favorite Stories from the First 50 Years
of the Award-Winning News Broadcast*

This Just In: What I Couldn't Tell You on TV

The Acting President
(with Gary Paul Gates)

SONGS

"There to Here" (with Jean Bratman)

"TV Anchorman"
"Little Lulu and Sister Hot Stuff"
"Longshot Love"
"Dark and Stormy Night"
(all with Diana Quinn)

BOB SCHIEFFER'S
AMERICA

Bob Schieffer

G. P. PUTNAM'S SONS

New York

PUTNAM

G. P. PUTNAM'S SONS
Publishers Since 1838
Published by the Penguin Group
Penguin Group (USA) Inc., 375 Hudson Street, New York,
New York 10014, USA • Penguin Group (Canada), 90 Eglinton Avenue
East, Suite 700, Toronto, Ontario M4P 2Y3, Canada (a division of Pearson
Canada Inc.) • Penguin Books Ltd, 80 Strand, London WC2R 0RL,
England • Penguin Ireland, 25 St Stephen's Green, Dublin 2, Ireland
(a division of Penguin Books Ltd) • Penguin Group (Australia), 250
Camberwell Road, Camberwell, Victoria 3124, Australia (a division of Pearson
Australia Group Pty Ltd) • Penguin Books India Pvt Ltd, 11 Community
Centre, Panchsheel Park, New Delhi–110 017, India • Penguin Group (NZ),
67 Apollo Drive, Rosedale, North Shore 0632, New Zealand (a division of
Pearson New Zealand Ltd) • Penguin Books (South Africa) (Pty) Ltd,
24 Sturdee Avenue, Rosebank, Johannesburg 2196, South Africa

Penguin Books Ltd, Registered Offices:
80 Strand, London WC2R 0RL, England

Library of Congress Cataloging-in-Publication Data

Schieffer, Bob.
Bob Schieffer's America / Bob Schieffer.
p.   cm.
Collection of commentaries: Schieffer's "final thoughts," with which he closed
his broadcast on *Face the Nation*, beginning in 1994.
ISBN 978-0-399-15518-5
1. United States—Politics and government—1993—Anecdotes.   2. United States—
Social life and customs—1971—Anecdotes.   3. National characteristics, American—
Anecdotes.   4. *Face the Nation* (television program).   I. Title.   II. Title: America.
E839.5.S29   2008   2008012790
973.92—dc22

Printed in the United States of America
1   3   5   7   9   10   8   6   4   2

BOOK DESIGN BY AMANDA DEWEY

For the two women I owe most, my loving wife, Pat, and my mother, Gladys Payne Schieffer, a child of the Great Depression who was determined that her children would have what was denied her, a college education. I became the first on either side of the family to graduate from college, and I believe she would be pleased to know that by 2008 not only had all three of her children graduated but her three grandchildren as well, amassing among them nine graduate and undergraduate degrees.

How can I know what I think till I see what I say?

—E. M. FORSTER

CONTENTS

V. LIFE, LIBERTY AND THE PURSUIT OF NEWS   91

VI. WAR AND PEACE   115

X. THE LIVES WE LED   *215*

XI. THE UNTHINKABLE   *233*

PREFACE

—————

This is a book of short essays about life, liberty and the pursuit of news. The vast majority of the pieces found here were the "final thoughts" that I began writing in 1994 to tack on the end of our *Face the Nation* broadcasts. "Final thoughts" is a misnomer, of course. If writing these pieces has taught me anything, it is that no thoughts should be final, especially mine. While most of them were written over the last fourteen years, a few of the somewhat longer ones go back to the 1970s, when I wrote weekly opinion pieces for CBS Radio.

Within this collection is to be found everything from reflections on war and peace to advice to fathers on how to "act normal."

The partisans of the hard right and left who seem to have no purpose but to prove the rightness of their cause will discover little of interest here. I find the professional screamers and their checklists of what constitutes a "liberal" or "conservative" predictable to the point of boredom. As I listen to their arguments on the cable channels and their unwillingness to give an inch on any issue, I still long for the day when someone on one side responds to someone on the other side by saying, "What an interesting point. You may be right." I'm still waiting, but I am not holding my breath.

I have always believed the greater and more intellectually challenging search is finding the things that bring us together rather than the differences that drive us apart.

In these essays, I have tried to follow the rule laid down by my great teacher Eric Sevareid to "elucidate, when one can, rather than advocate."

But I have tried, as well, never to forget his admonition "to retain the courage of one's doubts as well as one's convictions in this world of dangerously passionate certainties."

Most of the time, these essays are simply observations—snapshots of my thinking—about America and Americans and how we came to be who and what we are.

Over the years I have found more to celebrate than to lament about America. To be sure, there was plenty to criticize, including the failure of government in the wake of Katrina, the foolishness of a government bureaucracy so big and cumbersome that it sometimes was unable to get out of its own way and government in which political spin had become so ingrained that at times its officials could no longer even recognize the truth, let alone tell it.

But again and again, I would see evidence of the innate good sense and optimism that is so much a part of the American character. No matter the challenge, somehow Americans have always been willing to meet it, and somehow we have always found a way. That part has never changed.

I became moderator of *Face the Nation* in 1991, but the first of the Sunday commentaries did not appear until an April Sunday in 1994, on the weekend after Richard Nixon died.

On that Sunday, we covered the news of the day as we always did, then a panel of Nixon's aides reminisced about the highlights and lowlights of Nixon's time in the White House. I felt the program that day needed "a button," as we call it in the trade, a sentence or two that sums up or puts in context what has just been seen and heard. So I wrote the following and read it at the conclusion of the broadcast:

> *We end this morning with a personal note. Richard Nixon had been around so long he had become as much a part of the American landscape as the Washington monument. Now that he's gone, it's a little like looking out the window and discovering the*

monument is no longer there. It's going to take all of us a little while, I suspect, to adjust to the new landscape.

Nixon did some grand things and he did some dastardly things that greatly disappointed those who had placed their trust in him. But Richard Nixon's life is a reminder that we can learn from the imperfect as well as the perfect. Richard Nixon left the White House in disgrace, but he left the Earth with dignity.

This was before the days of e-mail, and over the next two weeks those few sentences generated more letters than anything or anyone who had appeared on our broadcast. Several weeks later, I tried it again, with similar results. In the coming months we offered brief commentaries during slow weeks when the news allowed, and by 1995, the commentaries were becoming a regular feature.

As the months passed, I began to worry that I might not have the authority to be offering commentary. CBS News standards are strict about expressing opinion in news stories, of course, and no one had done regular commentary on one of our hard news broadcasts since Eric Sevareid back in the 1970s.

Andy Rooney speaks his mind on *60 Minutes*, of course, but Andy has always marched to his own drummer, and I wasn't sure my marching orders allowed me to stride down the trails that Andy took. (Did you ever wonder if you had the same rights as Andy Rooney?) I finally decided that if I was violating standards, someone in New York would call and tell me to stop, and since no one called, I just kept writing. Then one day in 1996, the *Face the Nation* essays won a national Sigma Delta Chi award and the phone lines from CBS headquarters started ringing. "Great work," came the word from the high command. "Keep it up!" So I did.

As best I can tell, I have written somewhere in the neighborhood of seven hundred since then, but many of the program transcripts from those early years, when I was still writing them on an occasional basis, have been lost, so we may never know exactly how many there were. In any case, it is of no matter. Neil Nyren, who edited my memoir, *This Just In*, and I went through all of them and selected nearly 171. The truth is, the winnowing process was not all that difficult. One of the sobering things in looking back over the body of one's work over a period of years is to realize that not every piece stands the test of time, even a short time. Some thoughts that seemed important at the time, proved unimportant within months, sometimes weeks. Other times, I would stay on the same subject from week to week and become repetitive. During my campaign finance reform phase, I wrote about the subject so often, my wife, Pat, finally said, "Enough. You've convinced me, go on to something else!" She was right, of course, but the other part is the campaign finance mess is worse than ever.

Sometimes over the years I was too flip when I should have been more serious, too serious when seriousness wasn't required, and sometimes I was just wrong. I believed that President Bush had no choice but to disarm Saddam Hussein and that going to Iraq would bring America together. That didn't happen, and I came to believe we went to the wrong place with the wrong plan to fight the international war on terrorism. But I also came to believe that, once there, a rapid withdrawal of our forces would lead to an even worse situation than the one in which America found itself as we headed toward the 2008 elections. I have included some of these commentaries in this book, if for no other reason than to help me understand how my thinking evolved.

On lesser matters, I more often used the needle rather than the sledgehammer as my weapon of choice, though I once called Barry Bonds a jerk, and there is nothing subtle about that, I suppose.

In the introduction to a collection of his own commentaries, Eric Sevareid once said, "These hecklings from offstage are offered in the hope that, as footnotes to the history of our times, they may illuminate, occasionally instruct and entertain, or at the least, start a few arguments."

I have no such hopes. I will be happy if these pieces evoke simply an occasional smile or perhaps cause a reader to pause here and there and say, "I really never thought of it that way before."

These are just my thoughts, dear reader, and you are welcome to them.

I

HOW WASHINGTON
WORKS—AND DOESN'T

The truth is, Washington does work. If it didn't, most of us would be leading far different lives under far different circumstances. But watching the process too closely can be a nerve-racking, wrenching experience. Washington doodles and dawdles, makes too many excuses, takes too much credit where none is due, avoids blame where possible, spends too much time on the frivolous, too little time on the substantive, not nearly enough time trying to limit waste, speaks a language that by design few outsiders understand, seldom learns from its mistakes, but in the end generally gets it right.

As I have watched Washington from within for nearly four decades, I have seen it become meaner, more partisan and less productive, but here is the good news: the founders devised a system so ingenious that even the most incompetent who have come here have never been able to damage it beyond repair. America continues to move forward.

During 9/11, Washington found a way to put partisanship aside and pass a $40 billion appropriation bill and do it unanimously. That is the other good news: when it has to, Washington always finds a way.

I have tried to remember that as I watched the events unfold that are described in this chapter. Believe me, it wasn't always easy.

The key to understanding Washington is understanding who's who. It took a while, but in 1976, I outlined a guide on CBS Radio.

Big Shots

To get along in Washington, you have to know who the big shots are. That used to be easy. The big shots were the ones with the shortest titles—President, Secretary of Defense, Secretary of State.

The little shots had the longest titles—Deputy Assistant to the Special Assistant for Deputy Assistance. That sort of thing.

The big shots were also the ones who drove around in those big limousines and got invited to all those embassy parties. The problem is that with the proliferation of the federal bureaucracy now, everyone above the level of Deputy Assistant Gas Meter Reader gets a government car and many get a chauffeur to drive it. And there are so many embassies in Washington now that the big shots, little shots and middle shots are in social demand.

Even so, there are still ways to tell the big shots from the little shots. One way to tell is to watch them when they walk and not when they ride. Big shots never walk alone; they're always accompanied by aides. The big shot walks down the center of the hallway; the aides fan out in his wake in a formation not unlike a gaggle of geese heading south. If you are a really big shot, like the president, at least one security man will be moving along ahead of you like a minesweeper clearing the way for a battleship. Otherwise, the big shot is always the point man for corridor movements.

The big shot is also the one who is always walking empty-handed.

Aides always carry at least one piece of paper; usually a briefcase. The Deputy Assistant Secretary of Commerce will usually have two aides trailing him; an assistant Secretary of Defense will usually require six to seven aides in tow, at least two in uniform.

High-ranking military men generally have at least one colonel to carry the briefcases with all the charts and graphs.

When they go to Capitol Hill, the colonel who carries the briefcase sometimes does double duty, collecting the generals' hats and seeing to it they are tucked away safely in the hat rack so the generals can turn full attention to the charts.

Another way to tell the big shots from the small shots in Washington is to observe the way their mail is handled. Those at the bottom of the pecking order open their own mail and answer it. One step up in the pecking order, a secretary opens the mail and types up the answer as dictated by the fellow who got the letter. One step above that, an administrative assistant frames a reply to the letter, and presents that to the recipient along with the original correspondence. One step above that, aides sift through the letters and decide which letters the recipient ought to see; the others are answered by someone else. One step above that, aides read the incoming mail, answer it, and a machine signs it with the recipient's personal signature. The recipient then gets a summary report on the mail he has received and a brief report on how he answered it. Only a few letters that the real big shot gets will ever be seen by him personally.

The ultimate way, however, to tell the big shot is to find out how he gets his news. You and I, of course, just watch TV, read magazines and the newspapers. The lower-level bureaucrats do that, too.

The big shots don't. Depending on how high you are in the government pecking order, you get (1) a prepared summary on your desk each morning of what was in the newspapers and on TV the night before; (2) a videotape replay of selected excerpts from the TV that might be of interest; or, finally, (3) when you're far enough up the totem pole, a group of staff members are assembled each morning in your office to tell you not only what was in the papers and on TV, but what it all meant.

All of this sounds a bit ridiculous to the average taxpayer, of course, but there are certain advantages. After all, when they are sitting around in those government offices explaining to each other what was in the morning paper, they aren't out burning up a lot of gas in those government limousines.

—September 3, 1976

One thing that never changes: the Washington players find ways to take a bow whether or not they've done anything to deserve it.

Victory Over What?

I t was on Thursday last that White House officials and congressional leaders emerged from eight days of closed-door negotiations and announced with great fanfare that they had finally reached agreement on a budget to run the government.

At both ends of Pennsylvania Avenue, this was hailed as a great achievement. At the White House, the president and the Democrats fell over each other in self-congratulation as Republicans traded compliments at the Capitol. Between backslaps, each group summed it up as a victory for the American people.

Well, pardon a smart-aleck question, but a victory over what?

Congressional sloth and ineptitude? White House monkey business? Congress has been here since January and done virtually nothing. The president? Well, he has been busy, but why all the celebrating? Because they finally did, behind closed doors, what they should have been doing all year in public?

Should we be heartened that in the rush to go home and campaign for themselves they closed a deal so haphazard that neither side was really aware of the details of what they had agreed to and still don't know, apparently?

In a CBS News poll last week, three-quarters of the American people could not remember a single thing this Congress had done. Well, that's understandable, but it's not all bad. Most of what's been going on around here is best forgotten.

—*October 18, 1998*

Every so often we are reminded how it used to be.

Slow and Bluesy

Congress adjourned before Thanksgiving and won't come back to Washington until next year, so it's hard to know what every member of Congress is doing these days.

But I see by the *New York Times* that when Senator Robert C. Byrd spoke last weekend at a Job Corps Center dedication back in his home state, he recited a long poem from memory, then turned to a piano player, asked him to play "Amazing Grace." "Play it slow and bluesy," he said, and he proceeded to lead the crowd in singing the hymn.

I don't know what poem it was, but it struck me it's been a long time since I've heard of a politician, any politician, reciting a poem or leading a crowd in song or doing anything else that might be considered fun, let alone inspirational.

But Senator Byrd is not just any politician. He turned eighty just before Thanksgiving, and he's a throwback to the pre-television days when politicians had to be entertaining to hold a crowd, when politicians wrote their own speeches and political events were participatory exercises, where the speakers and the audiences played off each other and had a good time doing it.

How strikingly different it usually is today, when a political rally is defined as three people in front of a television set and when most of the political oratory we hear comes from that off-camera voice on a thirty-second television commercial that tells us how awful the other candidate is and reminds us to send in our contribution if we want access to the candidate. Call me old-fashioned, but I'd rather hear a poem.

—*November 30, 1997*

Get Out the Shovel

With a war going on in Kosovo and an argument back home over spies, guns and money, Washington may have set some kind of record this week for gobbledygook, spin, finger-pointing, excuses and downright lies.

Well, here is where I tune out.

Anytime a politician begins an answer to any question by saying,

"It's important that we put this in context," that guarantees a shovelful of blather to follow.

Anytime a politician says, "We have to be honest with the American people," which always makes me wonder when it would be appropriate to be dishonest with the American people, and if a politician was, would he tell it?

Anytime a Republican refers to the Democratic Party as the Democrat Party. Call them by their right name, guys; they don't call you Repubs.

Anytime the White House starts defining words, no recent examples needed. *(We were in the middle of that intern business.)*

Anytime a president of either party quotes from the letters of little children.

And anytime the military argues you can judge whether a war is being won by the number of buildings being destroyed or roads and bridges that have been torn up. No disrespect, but I remember all those enemy headquarters we captured in Vietnam, and all those times we cut off supplies coming down the Ho Chi Minh Trail.

Rest assured, the government response to this tirade is already in the works. I hear it has something to do with first putting it all in perspective.

— May 30, 1999

Dogs and Cats

Congress is about to adjourn. I alert you to this because Congress does so little anymore you may not have realized it's been in session.

You can count this Congress's accomplishments on your nose,

which ranks it on the "wonderful chart" at about the same place as the Congress before it. Which leads me to a cartoon I saw in *The New Yorker*. Two dogs are talking and one says to the other, "It's not just that dogs must win, but cats must also lose."

Well, that's our modern Congress. It has become so partisan that neither party will do anything if it means sharing credit with the other or unless it can be done in a way to discredit the other. So neither side gets anything done. Nonpartisan investigations have become impossible, bipartisan projects nonexistent.

Georgia's former Senator Sam Nunn, who is probably responsible for passing more significant legislation than any lawmaker of modern times, was in town this weekend, and it reminded me of something he said when he retired from the Senate four years ago.

"In all my years here," he said, "I never accomplished anything without the help of the other party."

Well, people around here just don't say things like that anymore, and come to think of it, Congress has accomplished virtually nothing since Nunn left.

—October 15, 2000

*We had just gone into Iraq, but this got me
worried about the home front.*

Tractor Man

W e were all awed by the power and expertise of the U.S. military last week, but if you live in Washington, as I do, that appreciation of the military may have been tempered by another thought: Does the government have any idea of how to deal with a terrorist attack back home?

After watching Washington authorities deal with a farmer who drove his tractor into a shallow lake near the Washington Monument last week, I have to wonder.

As Tractor Man threatened to blow himself up with explosives—and anyone with binoculars could tell he had none—he all but shut down a large part of this city for forty-eight hours. Traffic was tied up so badly that a hospital several miles away reported FedEx was unable to make deliveries and pickups there.

Had Tractor Man been an escaped elephant, he would have been shot with a tranquilizer dart and returned to the zoo in a matter of hours. Yet dozens of emergency personnel wasted two days holding a dialogue with him.

It was like the setup in a caper movie.

Thieves create a diversion, a fire or a wreck, and then steal the jewels while the cops are looking the other way. You had to ask: Are our emergency personnel so poorly trained they would fall for the same trick during a terrorist attack?

Maybe we should forget that stuff about duct tape and those

silly ads assuring us the government is doing everything possible to protect us and spend the money instead on realistic training and resources for our local authorities.

When one guy on a tractor can paralyze a big part of the nation's capital for two days, we've got a problem.

—March 23, 2003

Park Service Follies

The U.S. Park Service, the agency that guards our national monuments and takes care of our national parks, has come up with an idea to save money. The agency brass asked park superintendents to draft plans to close the parks on national holidays.

Yes, you heard right, close the parks on days when people are off work and have an opportunity to use them.

But that's just the stupid part. Here's the outrageous part. It turns out that one reason the Park Service is short of money is that Park Service officials have been doing a lot of traveling.

They spent $44 million on official travel at home and abroad just last year. And that includes stops in such exotic locales as China, South America, France and Italy.

Park Director Fran Manella was hauled before Congressmen Charles Taylor and Norm Dick's House committee last week and ordered to cut the travel and keep the parks open. She promised to comply. From now on, she said, no more overseas trips.

Well, that is a start, but it is just the latest chapter in a tale of Park Service mismanagement in which multimillion-dollar projects have been launched without congressional approval. In another incident, the Park Service police chief was fired for revealing she didn't have enough police officers to guard the national monuments.

So I have another travel tip. Give the Park Service brass their walking papers.

They shouldn't be out of work long. They can hire out as clowns.

—*March 28, 2004*

That one got me dropped from several Christmas card lists, but by 2007, the Park Service leadership had changed.

News item: In an exchange on the Senate floor, Vice President Cheney told Vermont Senator Pat Leahy to "Go f— yourself!"

The "F" Word

During the 1960 campaign, former President Harry Truman said the Republicans could go to hell. Candidates Nixon and Kennedy were asked for comment.

Nixon was highly offended by Truman's language. He said if elected, he hoped to maintain the standard set by Eisenhower, who had, in Nixon's words, "restored dignity, decency and good language" to the White House after Truman left.

Kennedy said he doubted he could do much to change the seventy-six-year-old Truman.

"Maybe Mrs. Truman can," Kennedy said, "but I don't think I can."

That's about where I come down on Vice President Cheney's now famous directions to Senator Leahy. The guy lost his temper. These things happen.

It's not the word that bothers me, but that we are seeing yet again an example of just how sour our politics has become.

Years of nasty, anything-goes campaigns have spilled over into the legislative process and poisoned the atmosphere so badly the two sides have trouble even identifying common goals.

Ask anyone on either side. They will tell you the partisan divide has grown so wide people in Congress no longer even know each other nor do they want to. Gridlock has become the norm in Washington.

Unable to make progress on major issues, the two sides spend endless hours bickering about small matters in order to torment each other for partisan gain—which is fine for them, but it's costing the rest of us a lot of money.

That's the obscene part.

—June 27, 2004

Every once in a while . . .

An Unusual Man

There is an old rule in Washington—never get between a politician and an open microphone, unless you want to be run over.

During the Clinton impeachment hearings, one member of Congress actually roamed the halls looking for microphones set up outside hearing rooms and upon seeing one would just walk up and start talking—even when there was no reporter there to conduct an interview.

Trust me, I saw it.

Which is why I call your attention to Maryland Senator Paul Sarbanes, who appeared only once on *Face the Nation*—one of the most unusual men ever to walk the halls of Congress because he never even seemed to notice the microphones there.

He said last week he'll retire when his current term is up and the reason was as understated as his career: if he ran again, he'd be eighty if he served his full term, and that's just hanging around too long, he said.

Sarbanes is a professional politician in a time when that is a pejorative term, but during thirty-eight years in elected office, what set him apart was that he never said much—the rare politician who let others take the credit to get things done, things like cracking down on corporate corruption.

Yesterday, one of his constituents praised him for just doing his

work and told the *Washington Post*, "He never came close to embarrassing us."

High and unusual praise in today's politics.

—*March 13, 2004*

The English Language
Debate

———————

I t's official! The Senate voted to make English the national language of the United States.

Do you feel a lot better knowing that? Or were you like me and
thought English was our national language?

Sort of like we know the Washington Monument honors George
Washington even though it doesn't have a sign on it that says Official
Monument to George Washington. Even I figured that one out.

Of course new citizens should speak English, but why would the
Senate spend hours debating whether to make English our national
language?

Let me break it to you gently: because it gives senators something to do while they avoid addressing the real problems—the war,
health care, the ballooning deficit and immigration, for that matter.

Working on real problems that have to do with national security and the country's fiscal well-being take determination, political
courage and the ability to compromise—all of which have become
the missing ingredients of modern politics.

So we'll hear more about silly issues between now and election
day, and come to think if it . . .

Maybe we should make the Washington Monument the national

monument to our first president, otherwise people might think it honors the Washington Airport.

And if senators designate Grant's Tomb the official tomb of General Grant, maybe that old joke about who is buried there would go away.

And while they're at it, maybe senators could declare the U.S. Capitol to be the national monument to wasting time and avoiding responsibility.

Actually, I doubt any of us needs to be reminded of that.

—*May 21, 2006*

Fighting Government Waste: An Act of Terrorism?

———

Are you tired of all those stories we hear on a daily basis about government waste, fraud and corruption?

Well, the *Washington Post* has discovered that the new head of the General Services Administration—a political appointee named Lurita Alexis Doan—has found a way to ensure we get more pleasant news.

She is trying to rein in her agency's independent inspector general, Brian Miller, whose tough audits produced those reports of government waste. She is trying to cut his budget by 5 million dollars. Mind you, he's watching over the 56 *billion* dollars in government contracts that the agency manages.

But you gotta love her reasoning. She claims Miller's tough reports are *intimidating government workers*. I can imagine!—especially the lazy ones who don't care where our money goes, and the occasional few who may be dishonest.

Ronald Reagan said in dealing with the Russians, "Trust but verify." Why shouldn't we be keeping tabs when billions are at stake here at home?

Ms. Doan seems to worry more about the auditors being disruptive. According to the *Post*, she told a staff meeting, "There are two kinds of terrorism in the United States—the external kind, and internally, the inspector generals."

For the record, she denies the quote, but as we put all this into our "You can't make this stuff up" file, we note highlights from her biography and that of her inspector general.

Before going into public service, she was a government contractor.

And, Inspector General Miller did have a connection to terrorism: he was once a federal prosecutor who helped bring the case against terrorist Zacarias Moussaoui.

—December 3, 2006

A Government That Can't Remember Anything

I have a travel advisory for visitors from outer space.

If you've been following the news lately, you can be excused for believing that government service is harder on human memory than Alzheimer's.

As the recent trial of Scooter Libby showed, White House work left him unable to remember anything.

But his problem was nothing compared to the epidemic of memory loss at the Justice Department, where federal prosecutors got fired. The attorney general couldn't remember talking to his own staff about the reasons why, whereas lower officials couldn't remember whose idea it was. And nobody at the White House could remember anything except they didn't do it.

Among the prosecutors who got fired was one who sent a Republican congressman to jail on corruption charges, another who did not push corruption charges against Democrats fast enough—at least not fast enough to please the Republican senator who complained.

Pressuring federal prosecutors to play political games is serious business. The president says he's not happy about it, and the attorney general says mistakes were made. Well, of course they were. But confirming the obvious is not enough. From the top down, the word must go out this will not be tolerated, and those responsible must be held accountable.

Even an alien from outer space can see that or smell it, because this one stinks to high heaven.

—March 18, 2007

If there is one thing Washington never does,
it is learn from past mistakes.

Lost Lessons from
Vietnam and Watergate

———

D oes anyone remember Watergate? Politicians found themselves in such low esteem that Jimmy Carter won the White House with a simple promise: I will never lie to you.

I remember thinking at the time, well, isn't that the least we should expect of our politicians?

But Americans had been told so many lies about so much, they had become suspicious of almost everything.

As I have watched events unfold in recent weeks in Washington—the army's cover-ups of the military hospital scandal and the facts surrounding the death of former NFL star Pat Tillman; and then the spectacle of an attorney general who can't seem to get his story straight on anything—I had to wonder, does anyone in a position of power these days remember what happened in those days after Vietnam and Watergate?

Well, I was there. They threw the Democrats out after Vietnam, and they threw the Republicans out after Watergate.

We learned then what too many seem to have forgotten now. Spin gets you only so far. Cover stories can be more dangerous than what people are trying to cover up. No media strategy can work unless it is grounded in truth, and "I don't remember" has never been much of an argument, either to my mother or to Congress.

If there is one thing that Americans won't tolerate, it is lying by those who hold positions of trust, which is why we call them positions of trust.

Why is it so difficult for the powerful to remember that?

—*April 1, 2007*

News item: A man who had been the object of a worldwide search because he was infected with a highly contagious disease was identified by a border guard, but was not detained because the guard decided to make his own diagnosis. And that was just part of it.

The Weirdest Week Ever?

Is it me or have we just come through one of the weirdest weeks ever?

For the record, it was the week a U.S. government border guard ignored a worldwide warning to detain that guy with possibly contagious TB and instead waved him through security "because he didn't look sick."

With all the talk about improving border security, maybe we should start by instructing government employees to read the directions.

It was the week that Barack Obama launched his religious

outreach website and we learned that he not only embodies Judeo-Christian values but also "the basic ideals and values of most Hindus."

Glad to hear it, but was that an issue?

In a shift, the president said he's ready to take the initiative on global warming because, he said, "science has deepened our understanding of climate change and opened new possibilities for confronting it."

Apparently, NASA Administrator Michael Griffin never got the memo and volunteered that it was "rather arrogant" to suggest global warming is a bad thing.

And then there was the story in the *Washington Post* saying that four years after the fall of Iraq, the United Nations is spending $10 million a year to train inspectors to search for Saddam Hussein's weapons of mass destruction.

Mind you, those same inspectors concluded before the U.S. invasion that there were no weapons of mass destruction. The invasion left them with no mission, but bureaucracies die hard and this one is still churning along—apparently because UN officials can't agree on how to shut it down.

What do you suppose we'll find out this week?

—June 3, 2007

If at first you don't succeed, change the subject.

When Defeat Is
Not a Victory

Before we get too far past it, some thoughts on the immigration reform bill that went down in flames last week.

The people who killed it—the politicians and the screamers on the left and the right—were calling that some kind of victory. Sorry. The legislation that went down had been loaded up with so much stuff it wasn't much of a bill anyway and probably should have been defeated. But what happened last week was no victory for either side or anyone.

It was just one more example of a White House that has frittered away its power and influence and a Congress that can no longer confront the nation's problems head-on and do anything about them.

Opponents killed the legislation, but there are still 12 million illegal immigrants in the country.

Any suggestions on what to do with them?

Opponents killed the legislation, but the security along our borders is still dangerously ineffective. Does anyone on either side believe that is a good thing?

Opponents killed the legislation, but the kind of highly educated, foreign-born specialists we need are still having a hard time getting work permits, and the hardworking immigrants who want to become good citizens will still find it difficult to realize their dream. What's to brag about that?

When nothing gets done, the politicians can always blame the other side. The bad news for the rest of us is the problem is still there.

—*July 1, 2007*

I've written more versions of this one
than I care to remember.

Nothing Doing
in Congress

———

S enate Republican Leader Mitch McConnell made a speech the other day in which he bragged that even though Republicans are the minority, they had kept many bad things from happening.

Well, that's just the half of it.

With the help of the Democratic majority, they have managed to keep much of anything from happening, good or bad.

Who says there's nothing that two sides can't accomplish together? Of course there is—doing nothing.

Congress ran to the airport Friday for yet another break—they're taking two weeks this year for Thanksgiving. I wouldn't ask how many days you're taking because that would be a digression.

But my question is this: What do the following have in common?

Legislation to provide health insurance for children, education legislation, energy legislation, the farm bill, funding the Iraq war and legislation funding all federal agencies except the Pentagon next year.

The answer is: all of them are stalled in Congress, awaiting final action, tangled in the gridlock that the Republicans blame on the Democrats and the Democrats blame on the Republicans.

Breaking the gridlock won't be easy. After all, once Congress gets back from the Thanksgiving break, Christmas vacation will be just weeks away.

I've heard all the excuses so many times, I've stopped listening. All I know is Congress continues to bring new meaning to that old phrase: nothing doing.

—November 18, 2007

II

VOTE FOR…
NEVER MIND

*I*t's no wonder I love politics. I grew up in a political family in Texas.

My mother was a Yellow Dog Democrat (she would vote for a yellow dog before she would vote for someone other than a Democrat).

The first politician I ever saw was Lyndon Johnson, who came to campaign on a vacant lot where we played ball in Fort Worth in 1948 when I was eleven years old and he was running for the Senate. My dad took me to see him because he came in a helicopter and we had never seen a helicopter.

My brother got a job while he was in college, working in the Capitol mail room for then-governor John Connally, and after finishing graduate school, was elected the youngest member of the state legislature.

He was and remains a Democrat, but I fell out of love with both parties years ago and became a registered Independent.

I kept my voter registration in Texas while my brother was in office so I could vote for him, but I vote now in Washington, and over the years I have probably voted for as many from one party as the other. I vote for the individual, not the party. (I once got so exasperated with the presidential candidates from both parties that I cast my ballot for Walter Cronkite.)

I may have problems with the parties and the candidates from time to time, but I never lost my love for politics or voting.

I'm like a cowboy around horses; they don't have to be good horses, cowboys just like to be around them. That's me on politics; I just like to think about it and be around it. But just because I love it, doesn't mean

I'm happy with our political system. To the contrary, I am worried about our whole electoral process and the way we choose our candidates. It's badly broken.

The primary system, which was designed to give more people a voice in the process, has given fewer people a voice—those who have large amounts of money to contribute to campaigns. It is the money people who get most of the say in today's campaigns. What was once an amateur sport has become a business for professionals—a business in which the cottage industry that has grown up around politics, the pollsters, planners, consultants, and ad salesmen, have become as important as the elections themselves. The campaigns have moved out of the community and onto the television screens. Public rallies are designed mainly to provide a background for television cameras.

The campaigns have become longer and more expensive, but can anyone argue they are producing candidates of a higher caliber than the old system?

If I had my way, I'd go back to the old system, junk the primaries, which gobble up the money, and do it the way we used to—select delegates at the precinct level, send them to the county convention to select delegates who would go to the state conventions, where delegates would be selected to send a state delegation to a national convention, where real political work would be done, the selection of a presidential nominee.

It wouldn't cost as much, it would restore spontaneity and even a little fun to the process, which would create public interest, and since the conventions would be making real news, the networks once again, and joined by cable, would give them extensive coverage. Here is a collection of my thoughts on that in recent years.

*Politics cost a bundle ten years ago, but the spending
back then wouldn't get a candidate far in
today's political world.*

McDonald's for President

A thought to consider as we begin another campaign year: candidate Bob Dole has already raised $25 million to spend on his
campaign; Phil Gramm, $20 million; President Clinton, who doesn't
even have a primary opponent, $26 million. Steve Forbes has already
spent $7 million, perhaps $12 million, most of it his own money.

Politics has become so expensive even those staggering sums no
longer cause comment.

The other day Charles Black, a respected Republican strate-
gist and consultant, actually said, "We ought to be spending more.
McDonald's will spend more to advertise hamburgers this year than
all the candidates together will spend on campaign ads."

*In 2008, Black was managing the campaign of John
McCain, onetime champion of campaign finance reform.*

It is an apt comparison in an era when candidates are marketed
like hamburgers.

But no matter how much money it burns up and how much business it brings to the professional consultants, the problem with selling candidates like fast food is this: when we opt for fast food, we sacrifice quality for convenience. Instead of the best, we often settle for what we can get quickly with as little effort and thought as possible.

The next time we complain about the kind of people who seem to be winding up in public office these days, we should ask ourselves: Has our acceptance of fast-food marketing techniques in politics lulled us into accepting fast-food quality standards when we go to the polls?

—*January 21, 1996*

Fact checks are always a good thing.

Debating Debates

When a viewer wrote in recently wondering why the candidates don't hold old-fashioned debates anymore, the kind they used to hold with a lot of back-and-forth, it piqued my curiosity about just what those early debates were like.

Well, a quick check showed they were not like anything because there weren't any.

Maybe because I'd forgotten my high school history, I had to be reminded that candidates didn't really campaign for president through a good part of the nineteenth century. It was thought beneath the dignity of the office.

The reason we tend to forget that, perhaps, is because we've heard so much about those famous Lincoln/Douglas debates. We also have to be reminded they weren't part of a presidential campaign, Lincoln and Douglas were running for the Senate.

What did set those debates apart is that, until then, most debating took place on the floor of the House and the Senate. Politicians seldom faced off anyplace else.

It turns out the first presidential debates between candidates didn't really come along until radio had been invented. Republican Tom Dewey debated Republican Harold Stassen over the airwaves.

The first real debate of candidates from the major parties was that 1960 Kennedy/Nixon encounter, and there wasn't another for seventeen years, until Jimmy Carter and Ronald Reagan met.

Well, just because they're a new idea doesn't mean they're a bad idea.

On the other hand, with the turn that modern campaigns have taken, maybe there is some merit in that nineteenth-century idea of just having the candidates stay home.

—*October 13, 1996*

Maybe it was something I ate the night before…

Just a Dream

I nodded off the other night as I was reading in the *New York Times* about how President Clinton had been telling Vice President Gore that the way to win the election was to lighten up, to relax, to get out of that blue suit and switch to sport shirts when he campaigned.

Well, soon I was dreaming and another presidential candidate was telling me about his strategy. I couldn't tell if he was a Democrat or a Republican, but he did have an unusual approach. Instead of going through all those polls about what to wear and what people want to hear, he said he was just going to tell everyone what he believed.

Then he said if enough people agreed with him, he'd keep on running. But if they didn't, he'd have more time for sport shirts. For instance, he said, he'd tell people, "We've got to step on some toes if we're really serious about reducing teenage violence and fixing Social Security and HMOs and schools."

And if we want a first-class military, he said he was going to tell people they'd have to pay for it.

"But if you're really serious about all that," I said in the dream, "the gun lobby and the entertainment lobby will turn on you, not to mention the senior lobby and the insurance lobby and the liberals and the conservatives, and who knows who else."

"But that's why I'm running," he said, "to change people's minds. Otherwise, what's the point?"

One other thing he said, "I'm going to try to set a good example."

Well, about then, the dream began to fade, as dreams always do. I never could make out if he was wearing a sport shirt or a suit.

—*May 16, 1999*

I shouldn't have, but I did...

My Exploratory Committee

I have a dramatic announcement, my fellow Americans. I have decided to form my own exploratory committee.

I am doing this for two reasons: first, everyone else seems to be doing it; and second, when they do, people for some reason send them millions of dollars.

Now I have thought about this, and any way you cut it, it sounds like a good deal.

Like Mrs. Clinton, who is the latest to form an exploratory committee, I am going to explore running for office, too.

Maybe for president of Italy. I've never lived there, but I love the food.

I won't stop there, though. I'm also going to do some regular exploring, like Admiral Byrd, who went to the South Pole. Well, maybe not. I like sled dogs, but the South Pole is too cold for me. Maybe someplace warmer, though.

There has been one problem getting all this organized.

With so many people forming exploratory committees these days, it's been hard finding people to be on mine.

Every time I ask someone, they say, "Sorry, already exploring for someone else."

Anyhow, I've talked this over with my family. It's one of the hardest decisions we've ever had to make. But we've decided to go ahead with it. We have also decided that however it comes out, we're going to keep the money, so be generous.

Thank you for your support and have a nice day.

—*June 6, 1999*

My Friends, It Is with a Heavy Heart...

Two weeks ago, I announced that I was forming my own exploratory committee, first because everyone else seemed to be doing it and, second, I noticed that when they did, people seemed to send them lots of money.

I promised only one thing: to keep the money.

Well, the response has been humbling. Steve in Atlanta sent a dollar and asked to be remembered as an early supporter.

William in Finksburg, Maryland, said he wanted to add his two cents' worth and sent exactly that, two cents.

Gordon in Oklahoma sent a dollar with strings literally attached.

Phyllis and Paul encouraged me to explore the South Pole.

Frank in Fort Worth promised an Italian coin, since I said one of the things I might explore was running for president of Italy.

David in Mississippi promised to visit me in Italy if I did get elected president there.

I must also report that some kind souls out there apparently thought I was serious and sent in money, too.

In all, we raised about two hundred dollars. While I am flattered, it is with a heavy heart I tell you I'm not really running for anything.

It was fun while it lasted, but the exploratory committee is closing down, and we will send back the money.

—*June 20, 1999*

The Industry of Politics

O n this Fourth of July, did you ever wonder what the founders would have thought of us, our generation?

Surely they would have been impressed with the wealth of America as it approaches the millennium. Certainly they would have admired the courage of what Tom Brokaw has called the greatest generation, our fathers and mothers who lived through the Depression and World War II.

But as I was thinking about the Clinton family scouring the country, looking for new offices to run for, and as I've been watching those congressmen trying to worm out of the promises they made to term-limit themselves so they can run again, I also wondered what the founders would think about the evolution of our politics; how we've developed an elite new class of professional office seekers and how that has spawned the enormous cottage industry of pollsters, consultants, advertising and media experts who reap billion-dollar profits from our elections, and how all that has made our politics so expensive that almost nothing matters but money anymore.

My friend Walter Mears, the Associated Press columnist, says he's been covering politics so long, he can remember when people worked in campaigns because they thought their candidate would be a good president.

These days, that motivates only some in politics, which, for so many, has become just another job. I think that's the part that would have astounded the founders.

—*July 4, 1999*

*Well, we learned a few new words
during the Monica era.*

Geeks and
Snolly-Gusters

———

Rummaging through a collection of Eric Sevareid's old commentaries, I suddenly realized what we're missing in this presidential campaign. We are sorely in need of more creative name-calling.

The best the Republicans have managed so far is when the *Manchester Union Leader* endorsed Steve Forbes, even though he "looks like a geek," as the newspaper put it. Now that's catchy, but we can't count that, since it was meant as a compliment, I guess.

No compliment was intended back in 1952 when Harry Truman called the Republicans "snolly-gusters," and Washington was so shocked then that Eric Sevareid had to remind his listeners that name-calling has always been a revered part of American politics. He remembered how General Winfield Scott's opponents called him "the peacock of politics—all fuss, feathers and fireworks," and how they said President McKinley had "the backbone of a chocolate eclair."

For pure invective, I have always been partial to John L. Lewis's description of Roosevelt's vice president Garner as a, quote, "labor-baiting, poker-playing, whiskey-drinking, evil old man."

Well, this year's Republican debates have been polite as a sixth-grade spelling bee, so if the Democrats want higher TV ratings for theirs, maybe Bill Bradley should start by calling Al Gore an "Internet-inventing, Love Canal–discovering, Earth-tone-wearing tree hugger." And what if Gore just called Bradley a "big dribbler" and then sat down?

Anyhow, if you hear of a candidate in either party who says his opponent has the backbone of a chocolate eclair, call me. I may vote for him.

—December 12, 1999

This was always one of my favorites.

The Joy of Voting

Several of my fairly famous colleagues have disclosed they no longer vote as a way of maintaining their neutrality as journalists. I admire their objective but I don't understand their reasoning.

Anyone who knows me knows how much I love my job, but it is a job. I wouldn't equate it with voting, which, to me, is my duty as a citizen, like paying the water bill.

I remember reading *The Rise and Fall of the Third Reich* as a young man and how surprised I was to learn the Nazis had used an election as a springboard to power. Had I lived in Germany then, I hope I could have voted against them. I wouldn't have wanted to be neutral on that one.

Besides, voting is just so much fun.

As a reporter, I have to back up what I say with facts. But I need give no reason, marshal no argument for why I voted the way I did. Maybe I just didn't like the candidate's attitude. That's reason enough to vote against him, or maybe I found a candidate who really is qualified. That's a good reason to vote for him.

It is my vote and I can exercise it any way I choose, but no candidate gets my vote unless I believe he or she deserves it.

We take voting so seriously at my house, my wife has instructed me not to tell even her whom I vote for. She's afraid I'll disappoint her. Oh, ye of little faith. But isn't that the best part? We can tell everyone or no one.

So go vote. It's good for the country and good for you. Makes you feel big and strong.

—November 5, 2000

*As the country waited for the Supreme Court to decide
who won the election in 2000, and waited and waited,
some worried about the short transition. That was one
thing I didn't worry about in those months.*

While Waiting for
a President

ome random thoughts as this presidential election continues to
sort itself out.

Number one: The country will survive. The only nation ever to
hold a presidential election during a civil war has a tradition and
respect for the law that is so strong it will find a way to get past this.

Number two: Don't worry about all this rush to get on with the
transition. Transitions were no big deal until the government started
paying for them. Jack Kennedy put together his entire administration in his Georgetown home. The prospective Cabinet members
were ushered in the back door, interviewed in the living room, and
those who made the cut were then brought to the front porch and
introduced to reporters, who waited out in the front yard. Not only
efficient, but cheap; Kennedy's daddy paid for the whole thing.

Three: In an unusual case like this, never try to figure out why
people do what they do. In the famous 1824 race that was thrown to
the House of Representatives to decide, John Quincy Adams needed
the vote of the state of New York to secure the majority required
to win the presidency. But the New York delegation was split. How
Representative Stephen van Resinlour voted would determine which

candidate got New York's electoral votes. Poor van Resinlour didn't know what to do and bowed his head in prayer. As he opened his eyes, he saw a ballot on the floor with Adams's name on it, took it as a sign from the Lord and voted for Adams. That swung New York behind Adams and gave him the presidency.

I have seen no sign of divine intervention this time, but the way this is going, maybe we'd best be on the lookout.

—December 10, 2000

The Supreme Court declared George Bush the winner of the 2000 campaign, but as 2002 dawned, that campaign seemed long ago—9/11 made it seem an event from another era, and perhaps it was.

What Was That Again?

A s the new year turned, I wondered what had been on my mind a year ago, so I looked up some of the stories I wrote back then. Mostly, they were about the long and strange presidential campaign.

What I didn't write about was foreign policy, and I certainly didn't write about terrorism. After all, it was a campaign year. And during presidential campaigns, we tell foreign policy to go sit in the corner and be quiet so we can all concentrate on issues that, quote, "touch people's lives"—or that's what we tell ourselves.

Frankly, I have a hard time remembering now what we talked about during campaign 2000. I remember John McCain was talking about campaign reform early on, but then he left. George Bush talked about reform with results, and Al Gore kept talking about that lockbox.

And there were competing plans about how we would spend that big surplus. Remember the big surplus?

In the press, we talked about candidates staying on message, but we didn't pay much attention to what the message was.

Sure, the campaign was about who could raise the most money, but that's old news.

What I find so striking a year later is just how irrelevant all of it was. Virtually nothing said in campaign 2000 was a predictor or a precursor of what would happen in 2001, nor did anything in that campaign really prepare us, or the new president, for what he would have to deal with.

Campaign 2000 did its primary job. It produced a new president, if just barely. But the rest of it was pretty much a waste. That's the fault of both parties and the press.

—January 6, 2002

Campaign Commercials

All last week I was thinking, What if someone from another planet came here and all he knew about our elections was what he learned from campaign commercials?

Well, first the alien would conclude that only the dregs of our society run for office, the liars, the thieves, the adulterers, even the occasional murderer, as I learned from one ad. I even saw an ad that accused a candidate of favoring public urination. The alien would also think that voter participation doesn't have much to do with voting but a lot to do with phoning candidates, as in call so-and-so and tell him to stop lying, or cheating or selling dope or whatever. How many times did we hear that one this year?

And, by the way, if you don't travel much, you'll be interested to know those ads on your hometown stations are like McDonald's. Go to the next town and they're just the same—the same accusations, the same grainy photos, the same raspy off-camera voice. Only the name of the person being attacked has been changed.

Campaign ads have been dumbed down now to the level of professional wrestling, the difference being that wrestling is occasionally funny. Are the ads effective? I can't imagine anyone taking them seriously. But the candidates must think they work. They keep paying for them. I guess we should also remember that wrestling does get high ratings on TV. And some people even believe it's on the up-and-up.

Well, here's the shame of it. Some won and some lost, but there were some fine people running this year. Too bad we couldn't tell it from their commercials.

—November 10, 2002

You gotta have sources.

Presidential Predictions

I just could not believe it when I saw in the paper that Pat Robertson said God had told him George Bush was going to win the election, and not just win but win in a blowout, a walk.

Gee, I thought, the president does look pretty strong right now, but if God starts leaking these results eight months before the election, these races aren't going to be much fun and it will be hell on Earth for the candidates. If people know who's going to win, the candidates won't be able to raise a dime and they won't be able to buy TV commercials and that could put the whole economy in the dumper.

Well, not to worry. I think my heavenly sources are just as good as Pat Robertson's, and my source says there was nothing to this story. He says, "Robertson must have misunderstood."

The way my source explained it, "God does know who's going to win all right. He knows everything. But," he said, "God would never tell that kind of thing. It would ruin all of it.

"He wouldn't tell that any more than he would tell the winning Powerball numbers," he said. And he said, "You have no idea the kinds of deals people try to make with God to get those numbers."

I thought that's how it was, but it's sure good to get it from a source at the highest level.

—January 4, 2004

*And I thought the commercials were the worst things
about campaigns....*

Campaign Ads and
Brain Waves

———————

T he story was right there on the front page of the *New York
Times*, but I am still not sure I believe it.

Political consultants have hired medical researchers at UCLA
to give people MRI exams to measure their brain waves. Why? To
gauge their reaction to campaign commercials. They haven't figured
out yet if Republicans and Democrats have different kinds of brains,
but they have determined that they seem to react differently to campaign commercials.

When Democrats, for example, saw those Bush commercials
that showed coffins at Ground Zero, there was activity in the part
of their brains that senses threats, as if Democrats subconsciously
believed the commercials would help the president. The Republican
reaction was more passive.

The consultants believe reading brain waves will help them know
in advance how people will react to their campaign ads, putting science into political science, they say.

Well, isn't that swell? If Franklin Roosevelt and Winston
Churchill had based their warnings about the Nazis on brain wave
readings of their people, they might have remained silent because
no one wanted to hear what they were saying in the beginning. They
wouldn't have remained silent, of course. As men of courage, they

knew there was no choice but to tell people what they did not want to hear. And would Lincoln have rewritten the Gettysburg Address if he had known in advance what the audience reaction was going to be? I doubt it, because he wanted to express his ideas, not the audience's.

What the researchers are missing here is that the whole point of politics, the whole point of government, is to improve the lives of the governed. There is no other reason for it. Reading brain waves won't add science to politics. It's just another scheme to figure out how to tell people what they want to hear, not what they want to know or need to know.

—*April 25, 2004*

As much as I was bothered by the turn politics had taken, as much as I was worried about the impact of money and the silliness and the nastiness, when the next campaign season came around, there I was back in New Hampshire and loving it.

Axes, Pancakes and Big Rigs . . . Oh My!

Here we are back in New Hampshire—sooner than ever but not too soon.

The way these other states keep moving their primaries up, New Hampshire may have to hold this year's contest before Christmas if it wants to be first.

Whenever it happens, what I love about New Hampshire is the wackiness it always brings out.

Like back in '84 when Democrat Gary Hart showed that he could throw an axe better than anyone.

Now there's a skill that every president needs.

Then there was George Bush's dad in '88. Someone accused him of being a prissy sort of a wimp, so he countered with a strategy of driving things with big wheels: forklifts, snowplows, tractors. He even got aboard an eighteen-wheeler and gave the horn a big toot. It worked: better images through heavy machinery.

And then there was the greatest unintended sight gag in the history of politics when Republican candidate Gary Bauer entered the pancake-flipping contest. He flipped his pancake high into the air . . . and then . . . and then . . . he fell right off the stage.

Bauer also dropped off the political map after that, but, except for his feelings, he wasn't hurt.

Yes, I've said it a thousand times, these campaigns start too early and they cost too much. But when you think about all the stuff that has happened here, you gotta love New Hampshire.

—August 26, 2007

III

THE BEST POLITICIANS
MONEY CAN BUY

*C*ampaign 2004 cost over a billion dollars. In 2008, spending in just the presidential race alone will surpass that figure. Bill Clinton had amassed a campaign war chest of $3 million when he ran in the New Hampshire primary in 1996. His wife had collected a staggering $100 million before New Hampshire rolled around in 2008.

Money was always a part of politics, but it has become the overriding factor in modern campaigns.

No candidate, no matter how brilliant or charismatic, can get elected without the money to buy campaign commercials. Only those who are willing to spend a major part of every day asking others for money can even hope to be elected. Since a vast part of the American people wouldn't even think of spending their days that way, we have come to see a different kind of person run for office, people who are willing to do just that. They are not bad people to be sure, some of them are very good people, but they are more akin to development officers and professional fund-raisers than those who sought office in the past, and with the new breed has come new values and new goals.

In 2004, the average winning Senate campaign cost $7 million, which meant the candidate had to raise $3,196.35 every day including Saturday and Sunday of his or her six-year term. Ask a retired politician why he or she decided to get out of politics, and most of them will tell you they just couldn't take another day of relentless fund-raising. Others may tell you they just got offers to make more money. The influx of money into the system has made public office a stepping-stone to wealth. Candidates find they can make more money and exercise more *influence lobbying than they ever did as congressional representatives or senators.*

Will it ever change? If it does, change won't come easily.

The hardest laws to write are the laws regulating campaign finance. It's difficult to limit campaign spending without running afoul of every American's right to free speech.

But there is another reason: campaign laws are the only laws written by those who are being regulated—the politicians themselves. No politician or political party can be objective about such laws, one party or the other always holds a majority, and the majority always tries to write the laws to favor its side. Every Congress that I have covered since I came to Washington in 1969 has tried some kind of reform or at least paid lip service to it, as has every administration. Yet every election has cost more than the previous one. Politicians have become addicted to money in the way hardened drug-users become addicted to heroin or cocaine. They want to break the habit and they hate raising money, but they're afraid that if they don't, someone else will and they'll get beat.

In order to get elected, politicians must sign off with so many special interest groups before they come to Washington that once here, their positions are set in stone, they are unable to compromise, and without compromise legislative bodies grind to a halt.

True reform can only come from the grass roots, and only when voters come to realize the current system has produced a government that can nibble around the edges of major issues but is incapable of confronting major problems head-on.

Real campaign finance reform will never originate in Washington. There is just too much money involved.

As I reflected on the essays in this chapter, it struck me that not many of them required an update or a line of explanation or even a comment.

In a capital where some things change and others don't, the impact of money on politics has had a remarkable consistency. Every year it just gets worse.

Calling Mr. Jefferson

I thought this weekend before the Fourth of July would be a good time to call my old friend Thomas Jefferson. Knowing his love of gadgets, you won't be surprised to learn he got back to me on his flip phone.

I wanted to know if he was surprised by these latest shenanigans in Washington, and he said, "Of course not. We expected it. That's why we decided no branch of government should be trusted with all the power."

What did surprise him, he said, was that Americans had let money become the driving force in politics. "You could do a lot of good with what these fellows spend on campaigns," he said.

He always figured ideas should be the driving force, and said modern politicians might stumble on an original thought once in a while if they stopped polling to find out what people wanted to hear and instead took time to write their own speeches. "It's a good way to figure out what you think" was the way he put it.

He just chuckled when I asked about the pressures of holding office that so many modern politicians complain about. "Heck," he said, "we figured there was a good chance they'd hang us when we signed the Declaration, but we just did it and moved on."

His call-waiting was clicking now, but as we were hanging up, I realized the best part of calling Mr. Jefferson is he always agrees totally with everything I believe. I bet you'll find the same thing if you call.

—*June 30, 1994*

A Simple Plan

T he growing scandal of big money in politics has everybody talking now about how to reform the system.

Well, after reading about President Clinton traipsing up to New
York to star at the kind of big-giver fund-raising party he says we
ought to eliminate and hearing about the big Palm Beach party that
Republicans gave to thank people who gave them at least $170,000,
I got to thinking about how to reform the system.

Well, the plan I came up with is fairly simple: just write down
what you feel you can afford to give a political party and then give it
instead to charity.

A quick check turned up these options: a Washington group says
$170,000 will pay for a hot meal for more than a hundred thou-
sand homeless people for a year. For just $100, a group can feed fif-
teen poor people for a week. A community college in Maryland told
us that amount would pay one-year scholarships for seventy-three
students. A Washington shelter told us it could provide a year's food
and shelter for seventy-seven abused women for that. Just $500
would provide a night's shelter and food for eighty-four women. Or
you could buy seventeen thousand kids who need them a pair of
shoes.

People at recent Democratic and Republican fund-raisers seemed
nervous about the publicity they've been getting. Some at the Palm
Beach gathering removed their name tags to avoid being identified,
which reminds me that one of the nice features about my plan is all

the groups I contacted said they'd be delighted to keep your donation confidential.

—February 23, 1997

Sam Houston

———

Last week was a time of important anniversaries for those of us who were born in Texas, the week that 161 years ago Texans declared their independence from Mexico. It was in the same week that the Alamo fell, and fittingly the week Texans celebrate the birthday of Sam Houston, who led that ragtag mob that defeated the Mexican army and who later went on to become president of the republic of Texas and later its governor and senator.

As I was trying to keep up with all the lawyer talk this week that public officials were offering to explain their actions about how political contributions don't affect policy, about who called who from where and why they didn't really want to do it, but the other side does it, so they had to do it, it struck me how easily old Sam Houston explained the controversial stands he often took.

When big-money interests derided him for opposing legislation aimed at forcing the Indians off their land, Houston rose in the Senate with a simple explanation, "Sir, these people are friendless; they have no political influence, they have no hope, no expectations to offer to the ambitious and the inspiring." In other words, there was no one else to do it.

When Texas left the union over Houston's objections and the Legislature demanded he swear allegiance to the Confederacy, he refused, knowing it meant his certain impeachment. Again, he explained in simple terms. "I'm ready to be ostracized," he said. "The office has no charm for me that it must be purchased at the sacrifice of my conscience and the loss of my self-respect." And with that, he walked away.

But my guess is old Sam Houston was proud to tell those stories to his grandkids. I'm not so sure grandchildren could follow some of the complicated explanations we've been hearing lately.

—*March 9, 1997*

Needed: A Twelve-Step Program

I t was like trying to get a child to take castor oil, but reluctant Senate leaders finally cleared the way this week for a debate on setting new rules on how politicians raise campaign contributions.

The sponsors of the proposed legislation want to put limits on those huge donations of hundreds of thousands of dollars that flooded last year's campaigns.

President Clinton made an impassioned speech about how necessary it was to reform the system, then promptly went to a fundraising dinner designed to raise just the kind of unregulated, large campaign gifts the reform legislation is designed to eliminate.

"Gotta do it," the White House said. "We want to stop, but we can't stop until the Republicans stop. Can't disarm unilaterally."

Excuse me, but whatever happened to the concept of setting a good example?

What if the president just said, "This is wrong, so we're not going to do it anymore, and I dare the Republicans to do the same"? Or what if the Republicans made the same dare to the White House? Or what if either side promised to quit for ninety days if the other side would, and if that worked, take it day by day, the way people dry out from drugs or alcohol or any other addiction.

Because that's what we have here, an addiction, and the only people who can't see it that way are the addicts.

—September 28, 1997

All Things to All People

Forget Monica and all that. As I watched Bill Clinton's news conference Friday, it struck me how much he has come to exemplify the modern politician. He is charming, telegenic, master of fund-raising and focus groups. All the tools needed to get elected in the television age.

But as the epitome of the modern politician, he's also an example of what has happened to politics.

In his new memoir, and it is his best book yet, Henry Kissinger suggests the relentless pressure to raise money so they can campaign on television has left politicians no choice but to present themselves as all things to all people. It is a condition, he says, that leads to compulsive, personal insecurity, and causes politicians to be more interested in becoming superstars than heroes.

And as he rightly points out, there is a difference. Heroes walk alone. Stars seek public approval. Heroes are driven by inner values. Stars by consensus.

In Kissinger's view, the drive to maintain constant public approval has left our leaders unable to fill their most crucial role: to provide the emotional ballast when experience is being challenged by change. Which has led to a curious paradox, he says. Never have political leaders been more abject in trying to determine public preferences.

Yet in most democracies, respect for the political class has never been lower. I think the old professor may be onto something.

—March 21, 1999

The Washington Aquarium

D uring the campaign finance reform debate, Senator John McCain told the Senate money had corrupted the whole political process.

Well, several of his colleagues took great umbrage. "How," they said, "can you call a system corrupt if you can't name the individuals who have been corrupted?"

I have concluded their indignation was sincere, and to me, that's the worst part. Money has smothered politics to the point that the closer you are to it, the harder it is to see the changes it has wrought.

Here's an example: when I did a story a couple of weeks ago about the insurance industry throwing a $1,000-a-plate breakfast for House Speaker Dennis Hastert on the very day the House was beginning debate on the HMO reform bill, lobbyists and congressional aides kept asking me, "Why are you making such a big deal of this? It happens all the time." Well, yes, I thought, but isn't that the point?

I did understand their question, though. After all, the way the lobby throws around money, a thousand bucks isn't much to them. Or to the politicians who collect it. To the insiders, it is routine.

But take a step back and even a child might ask, why would anyone pay $1,000 to have breakfast with a politician if they didn't want something? The bacon and eggs on Capitol Hill just aren't that good.

And that's the serious part. The situation has become so bad, those involved no longer understand what it's done to them. It's like a fish in water. It's such a part of their lives, they may be the only creatures who don't know they're wet. But the rest of us do.

—*October 24, 1999*

And speaking of fish, I filed the next commentary from
the Republican convention in 2004.

Casting the Line

We talked a lot last week about how the party conventions are no longer the place the candidates are chosen but where they are showcased.

What we didn't talk enough about is what else they've become: a central gathering point for corporate and special interests to buy access and lavish money on the elected officials who make the laws that govern our lives.

It has reached such obscene levels that even some of the politicians are offended. As Nebraska Senator Chuck Hagel surveyed the nine-hundred-plus fund-raising parties around Philadelphia, some of which cost as much as $400,000, he said, and we quote, "We are showcasing the things that are driving people away from politics." It would be hard to argue otherwise. Scores of corporations claiming to be interested only in good government have given more than a million dollars each to both conventions.

At one Philadelphia lunch, Republicans collected more than $10 million. Individuals who gave the party a quarter of a million dollars—yes, I said individuals who gave a quarter of a million dollars—joined corporate guests in private skyboxes. Officials were a little defensive when asked about it. The *Washington Post*'s Michael Allen was turned away from one party by an official who explained, "Guests might have people on their arms who weren't spouses." Don't believe I would have said that.

But camera crews who promised to be quiet were allowed to watch those who paid $5,000 to fish with House Speaker Dennis Hastert.

We heard the speaker say, "Don't want to scare these fish away."

Why would anyone want to pay to fish with a politician?

Our camera crew interviewed one of the fishermen, who said, "Whether you're for the airline industry or for the insurance industry or whatever industry, this seems to be the way things get done."

As absurd as it has become, we should not be surprised. Conventions reflect the reality of modern politics. It's mostly about money and little else.

To make sure he gets every dollar that's left, Democrat Al Gore took no chances when it came to picking someone to run his convention next week in Los Angeles. He didn't turn to a politician. He picked Bill Clinton's top fund-raiser.

—*August 6, 2000*

A Real Debate

I tried to get the *Evening News* to do a story last week about how the Senate was having a real debate on campaign finance reform.

Well, I kept getting turned down, and then I understood why. Like most people, the editors in New York assumed the Senate has real debates all the time. I have a scoop for you. The Senate hardly ever has a real debate.

You can usually tell how a senator is going to vote by checking who contributed to his or her campaign. By the time issues get to the Senate floor, everything has been worked out, all sides generally know how the vote is going to end up, and debate, if you want to call it that, usually amounts to no more than senators reading speeches written by someone else to an empty Senate chamber. The key word here is "boring."

Well, that's until last week. Republican leaders have always blocked campaign finance reform from coming to a final vote, but in a Senate divided 50-50, that's no longer possible. So with a filibuster no longer a question, individual amendments are being debated and voted on, and no one knows which amendments will be considered until they're introduced on the floor.

So the debate has been spontaneous, and compromises are being struck, and legislation is being written, well, like it's usually portrayed in the movies. What has surprised the senators is that they love it. It's been so long since they've had a real debate, they had forgotten how much fun it can be.

I'm with them. I don't know how this one is going to come out,
but campaign finance is finally getting the airing it deserves and the
Senate has never looked better.

—March 25, 2001

I wrote this in the weeks after 9/11.

Bad Advice vs.
Common Sense

———

P residents get a lot of advice; happily they don't always take it.
     Case in point, the Republicans were planning a big politi-
cal fund-raiser this week in Washington. It had been planned long
before the attack on the Twin Towers, and President Bush was to
have been the star attraction. Those who chipped in $100,000 or
more were even promised a photo with Mr. Bush.

Well, here's the part you may find hard to believe: the president's
political team was telling him last week that he should not change
his plans. War or no war, they told him, he should go.

It apparently caused quite a behind-the-scenes set-to in the
White House. According to the New York Times—and we are not
joking here—the political advisers said, quote, "There is a powerful
argument that if you really want the country back to normal, politics
and fund-raising are part of America."

Well, so is stupidity in some quarters, but do we really want to encourage it?

And wouldn't it have looked swell, the president out running around in a tuxedo getting his picture taken with the money boys while our pilots are risking their lives in Afghanistan and postal workers are dying from anthrax?

To his credit, President Bush rejected the advice and decided to stay home and run the government. Good for him.

And wouldn't it be great if that became the rule, that presidents ran the country and left the money grubbing to others? After all, if they run the country right, they won't need to raise any money.

—*October 28, 2001*

The Money Game

I was watching CNN the other day when North Carolina Senator John Edwards made his announcement that he'll run for president.

As these things go, it was a perfectly fine announcement. He talked about fighting for regular people, about the economy, about trouble overseas. But the first question he got from reporters was not about any of that. It was this: How much money have you raised?

That's what we've come to in politics. Money has become such an overpowering factor that even the reporters are caught up in the money game. Who's got the most? Who's best at raising it? Sadly, money questions are pertinent because nine times out of ten, the candidate with the most money wins, because that's the candidate who can buy the most TV commercials. Even sadder, those commercials are where millions of Americans get most of what they know about politics.

After railing for years about money in politics, I've decided on a radical new course. I know it's radical, but what if those of us who cover politics paid less attention to who can raise the most money, and paid more attention to what these candidates are saying, more attention to the programs they propose and what impact, if any, these programs will have on our lives? Even more radical, what if we tried to find out the candidates' views on foreign policy? Who knows?

If we did a good job at that, if we gave voters enough solid information, maybe they wouldn't have to depend on those commercials to find out about politics. If that happened, the politicians would stop buying those commercials and the rest of us wouldn't have to listen to them. Now tell me that's not a good deal.

—January 5, 2003

IV

HAIL TO THE CHIEF

If I count the brief encounter I had with Richard Nixon (see details in this chapter), and I'm sure I'm the only one who counts it, I can truthfully say I have interviewed all seven men who have occupied the Oval Office since I came to Washington. I liked some of them better than others; some of them liked me, and I would guess some of them didn't. But that's beside the point and all in a day's work.

The presidency of the United States is unique. Harry Truman used to say, "I can send soldiers into combat, but I can't fix a traffic ticket." Truman was recognizing the checks and balances the founders built into our system, which prevents any part of the government or any officer of the government from monopolizing all the power of the government. If I might slip in a brief commercial for the First Amendment, Truman was also recognizing that a free press is always there to give its citizens its own version of what the government is doing, a version that does not always jibe with the government's version. Only in a democracy is that second source of information available, reason enough for a free press (end of commercial).

Everything a president does affects someone, somewhere. Everything the president says is news. So much power emanates from the Oval Office that as I was growing up, Americans believed it transformed those who held it. Truman was little known to the American people when he came to office, but I can remember my dad saying back then, "That office makes the man." After Roosevelt brought the country out of the Great Depression, we had come to believe that our presidents were invincible, superhuman. All that changed with the assassination of John

Kennedy. America lost its innocence during that awful weekend. We came to understand our presidents were not superhuman, but as vulnerable as the rest of us, and it shook our confidence. By the time I got to Washington in 1969, America was asking if the presidency was more than any one person could handle, and a chain of violence and scandal did little to restore confidence in the office or the government. The presidency had cost John Kennedy his life. The next president, Lyndon Johnson, was driven from office by an unpopular war, only to be succeeded by Richard Nixon, who was forced from office by the Watergate scandal, which brought Gerald Ford, our first unelected president, to power. He was defeated when he sought election in his own right; pundits said it was because he had pardoned his predecessor. That brought the little-known Jimmy Carter to the White House. He was defeated for reelection by Ronald Reagan, who would become the first president since Eisenhower to serve two full terms.

From Nixon on, I had a front-row seat to watch the presidency and the men who occupied the Oval Office. I traveled with them on campaigns and around the world. It gave me the opportunity granted to few Americans, a close-in vantage point to watch the effect the office had on our presidents and the imprint each of them left on the office.

Of them all, I liked Gerald Ford best, and it had nothing to do with politics. He was just one of the nicest people I ever met in public life. I also believe his pardon of Nixon, which I opposed at the time, was not only an act of political courage but vitally important to the nation's well-being—perhaps as important as anything that has been done by all of the presidents I have covered.

Watergate had brought the nation to a standstill. Ford understood before others that we needed a break to catch our collective breath and regroup. Watergate had gone on for two years and had come at the end of a long and decisive war that had nearly torn the country and its institutions apart.

As I watched the country go through the trauma of the Clinton impeachment, I came to understand what the impact on the country would have been had Nixon been indicted and brought to trial. It would have taken years, left the country even more divided and unable to focus on its problems at home and in a world that continued to grow more dangerous. America at the end of Vietnam and Watergate was a country whose patience and beliefs had been tested to the limits. We needed to rest and change the subject. Ford gave us that chance and understood the political price he would pay for it, but I believe it was the right thing for the country.

I have never been hesitant to criticize presidents or the government, but looking back on it, I have decided that only those who serve in the office can truly understand the complexity of the presidency—the relentless pressure, the round-the-clock scrutiny, the realization that nothing can ever be completely off the record, and that everything a president does has an impact on someone and that many times those decisions put lives at risk.

I had my differences with all the presidents I covered, but in each of them I found something to admire, even Nixon. He abused the Constitution and should have been impeached had he not resigned. But his diplomatic opening to China and his arms control agreements were magnificent achievements. He was far ahead of his party and the public opinion of his day, and he will be remembered for more than being the first president to resign from the office.

The dreary presidency of Jimmy Carter was seen by many as a failure, but the Panama Canal treaty that Carter negotiated was a major achievement, and the Camp David accords removed Egypt, the largest nation in the Arab world, as the main threat to Israel.

It was covering the presidencies of Ronald Reagan and Bill Clinton that taught me the greatest lesson: always give it a few years before you try to judge a president.

I wrote a book about Reagan that came out within months after he left office. Everything in that book remains correct, but it is no longer really accurate. When I wrote it, I had no way of knowing that Reagan's military buildup would trigger an arms race that would eventually plunge the Soviet Union into bankruptcy and lead to its collapse.

The breakup of the Soviet Union wasn't entirely the result of Reagan's policy, but it was certainly a factor, and that will surely be a part of his legacy. I could see no sign of that when I wrote that book in 1988.

For me, Clinton was the most disappointing of the presidents I knew. He was the most gifted politician I had encountered since Lyndon Johnson and one of the most charming people I had ever been around. I believed he had the skills to make a real difference, and he did get the economy rolling and the deficit became a surplus. When he became entangled in the Monica mess, my first reaction was that I simply couldn't believe it.

I never thought Clinton should be impeached. To me, that's a penalty to be reserved for those who try to topple the government or sell out America to a foreign enemy, but I did believe he should have been censured in some way.

I was not alone. Polls showed the American people did not favor removing him from office, and Senate leaders on both sides of the question said there never were enough votes in the Senate to remove him, but the Republicans who led the impeachment drive ignored the polls and the Senate vote-counters and demanded removal or nothing.

They got nothing. The Senate voted not to remove Clinton from office and he got no penalty. He "walked," as we used to say at the Fort Worth courthouse when a defendant was found not guilty.

Even so, I thought history would judge him harshly, as several of the essays I have included in this chapter reflect. On that, I got it wrong, at least in history's early version. Within months of leaving the White House, Clinton was listed as one of America's most admired persons. He became a millionaire many times over from the proceeds of a best-selling book, and within a year was the highest-paid speaker on the lecture circuit, drawing $150,000 to $200,000 per speech.

Campaigning for his wife when she declared for the presidency in 2007, he joked that rolling back the Bush tax cuts wouldn't hurt poor folks but rich people like him. He said he loved to say it because he hadn't been rich for most of his life.

In December 2007, a CBS News poll showed that the main thing voters liked about presidential candidate Hillary Clinton was that she was Bill Clinton's wife.

Americans are a forgiving people. I had underestimated just how forgiving.

Vietnam and Watergate had come and gone and Bill Clinton had become president by the time I started to write commentaries on a weekly basis for Face the Nation. In this section are some of my thoughts on Clinton and the president who followed. Nixon, Reagan and Ford died during that period, and I have included some thoughts on them as well.

Include Me Out

_____

When I was a little boy, my grandmother was certain I would be president someday. She was wrong, of course, but that's how people used to think of the presidency and the kind of dreams that they had for their kids and grandkids. How different it is today.

When Colin Powell told us this week that he did not want to go through the ordeal of running for president, most people nodded sympathetically and said they understood. When it became known that his wife worried for his safety, most of us said, "Who can blame her?" That is the most disturbing part: American politics has become so vile, the process of selecting a president so odious and dangerous, that good people in many cases just no longer want a part of it, and we have become resigned to it.

The next time you hear one of those sleazy political ads on television and wonder what kind of impact our mean politics is having on American society and the American psyche, ask yourself this question: How long has it been since you've heard a mom or a dad or a grandmother say, "Someday, I hope my son or daughter is going to be president."

—_November 12, 1995_

Me, Too

I n a recent commentary, we noted that the best way to understand the impact of mean and sleazy politics on our national psyche is to ask yourself how long it's been since you heard anyone express hope that their child would grow up to be president.

Well, that comment provoked more than the usual reaction, and the interesting and perhaps sad part is, virtually no one disagreed.

Richard Martinovich of Battle Creek, Michigan, said we didn't go far enough, though. That the media bears part of the blame. That many "public officials get eaten alive by the media feeding frenzy, so it is no surprise many qualified people decide public service is not worth it."

Barry Hayman, a high school government teacher in Genesee, Pennsylvania, wrote, though, to say, "Federal government is a hard sell to young people who see and hear elected officials who berate one another."

But he went on to say he thought his son and daughter would both make great presidents or Speakers of the House, and he said, "They already get along better than Bill Clinton and Newt Gingrich." I'll bet he's right about that, especially the last part.

—December 10, 1995

President Clinton took the oath of office for the second
time after months of partisan warfare that had at
one point shut down the government. We had no
idea there was even greater rancor ahead.

Second Inaugurals

S econd inaugurals are never as exciting as the first ones: the difference between a wedding and wedding anniversary, someone
said the other day.

Still, this will be the ninth one that I've been to, and I cannot
remember one where there's been less excitement, anticipation
or even talk about it. And the reason why may be more than just
second-time-around blahs.

Washington has changed. It's become a bitter place of scandal,
where partisanship runs more deeply than ever, the natural result,
I believe, of a campaign process that has come to be dominated by
a new class of professional strategists who are hired with only one
purpose: win at any cost.

The hateful atmosphere that now characterizes the modern
campaign has begun to spill over into the governing process itself.
Whatever spontaneity and excitement there once was in politics has
been squeezed out by the all-consuming need to raise the enormous
sums of money needed to finance the modern campaign. Where's
the pleasure in that, except, of course, for the professionals who get
the money?

Yet when the president is sworn in tomorrow, all will go as
planned. No one will try to stop the ceremony. We won't have to

check with the military to see if it's all right. Even the president's bitterest foes would not consider trying to install anyone except the person who got the most votes. There are still many places in the world where it would be unthinkable to do what we will do tomorrow, but our system of government was so cleverly designed and our values such that here it can be no other way. That is something to be excited about and what we really celebrate tomorrow.

—*January 19, 1997*

The scandal over Monica Lewinsky had begun
during those bitter days of the government
shutdown, but we would not learn of it until
the early days of the second term.

Role Model?

No one really expects a president to be entirely candid, to begin a news conference by saying, "Good afternoon. Here's a list of all the things I've done wrong." But over the years, presidents have gone to great lengths to convince us of their candor and that, if there were questions that they couldn't answer, there were good reasons for it—national security or some such.

Even Richard Nixon tried to appear candid. Of course, he had to lie to do it, which is why I was struck by President Clinton's theme at his news conference Thursday. He served notice early on that on some subjects, Monica Lewinsky foremost among them, he no longer finds it necessary to give reasons for not answering, and he didn't.

He has clearly concluded that, as long as the good times last, people won't demand answers about the other things, another way of saying presidents are elected to run the government and people don't expect much beyond that. In keeping with that, when a reporter asked him to what degree he thought a president was a role model in his private behavior, this was Mr. Clinton's answer: "Well, these are questions that you need to ask and answer without my involvement, for the simple reason that our consensus about that over time has changed dramatically," end quote.

That's the part that bothers me. The president's our highest elected official. We entrust him with powers and weapons that could destroy the world. When he says he's the wrong one to be asking about what constitutes a role model, it makes me a little nervous.

—May 3, 1998

Starskruck

Since we spent so much time last week going over the president's words to the grand jury, I decided to spend the weekend going through all the e-mail, letters and testimony that Monica Lewinsky gave to the jurors.

But I'm glad I did. Her tarty public persona aside, what struck me, as she bared her soul to the grand jury, was just how young she was, and for all her fast ways, how vulnerable she seemed.

Her worries were the worries of her generation. She worried about her weight, about being taken seriously. And, as she wrote to a friend, about finding someone someday who would just give her a hug.

Instead, she got tangled up with the president, she became a small part of his life. He became the center of hers. She'd let herself dream that they might have a future together, lived for the minute or two when he might say something nice to her. When he felt the need and summoned her, she always brought a little gift. One time she even brought a gift for his dog.

When he gave her little trinkets, she was beside herself. "All my life," she wrote, "everyone has always said I am a difficult person to shop for, yet you manage to choose absolutely perfect presents, gifts for my soul."

All that for a book of poems and some junk, but that's how it is when you're starstruck and hopelessly in love.

I know, I know, what she did was wrong, but I feel sorry for the kid.

—*September 27, 1998*

*As 1998 drew to a close, Washington was consumed
with impeachment talk and whether the president
should be removed from office. Over the next weeks I
offered my own thoughts—sometimes tongue in cheek,
sometimes not—on what should be done.*

Are We There Yet?

From what I'm hearing from House Republicans, they no longer believe they have the votes to impeach the president, but the question is: If they don't impeach him, should he be punished?

I think he should. I never thought the stuff he did warranted impeachment, but let's face it, it was pretty scummy stuff and a rebuke or censure would be letting him off too light. I'm thinking more along the lines of sending him on a long car trip. Instead of impeachment, the House of Representatives should load up a car with all the characters who put us through this mess and sentence the president to drive them across the United States.

Next to the president, I'd put Linda Tripp in the front middle seat, where she'd have access to the phone and the tape deck. Lucianne Goldberg, that New York woman who was always egging her on, would get the window seat. Ken Starr could sit right behind the president—a good place to give out driving tips. To keep the conversation going, how about Monica's old lawyer, Bill Ginsburg, next to him?

And to make sure Congress was represented, how about Barney Frank in the seat next to Ginsburg? If we could get a Suburban, Monica could sit in the way back with any number of lawyers from either side. Cruel and unusual punishment to be sure, but they'd all get to know each other just as we've come to know them. Who do you suppose would be the first to ask, "Are we there yet?"

—November 22, 1998

A History Lesson

Well, we've been talking history, so now it's time for the test. Here's what we're going to do. I'll say a name. You make a mental note of the first thing that crosses your mind. Are you ready? Here goes. Abe Lincoln. George Washington. Franklin Roosevelt. Babe Ruth. Or how about Thomas Edison? Now let's get back to politics. Bill Clinton. Yup, that's what I thought of, too.

That's why I don't buy this argument that he's going to walk away unpunished if Congress chooses not to remove him. Whatever Congress does or doesn't do, he still gets the worst punishment of all. You can't think about him without thinking about all of that.

It once occurred to me that our time would provide the trick questions for history tests of the future. Who was the first president to resign? Who was the first unelected president? The first unelected vice president? The second unelected vice president? Now we can add another question: Who was the first president to get caught having phone sex?

For the rest of his life, every time Bill Clinton passes a school where children are studying history, he'll get to think about how he became the answer to that question. That's not exactly beating the rap. Oh, and by the way, the second unelected vice president was Nelson Rockefeller.

—November 29, 1998

The Boy Who Shook
Hands with JFK

As I watched the Judiciary Committee hearings, I kept thinking back to that picture of a teenager named Bill Clinton shaking hands with President Kennedy in the Rose Garden of the White House back in the sixties.

Here was a kid who had come from almost nothing, who went on to spend his whole life wanting to be president, and against all odds pulled it off; only in America, as the cliché goes.

And there he was then, on television Friday, apologizing again. His message was that if only he had it all to do over again, he wouldn't. He recited the familiar lines about the moving finger, having writ, moves on.

Whatever one thinks of him, there was something pathetic, even sorrowful, about hearing someone who had spent his whole life trying to be president say that if Congress would just let him keep the office, he would sign a statement saying he had dishonored it.

What do you suppose that kid who shook hands with President Kennedy would have thought about all that?

—December 13, 1998

One Year On

It was a year ago this weekend that Kenneth Starr issued his report, but so much has happened since then, it seems to me as if it was ten years ago.

For me, it was one of those days I will never forget, the first time as a reporter that I was truly at a loss for words. I have always been one of those who believed there's not much that ought to be kept secret, but as I was reading the report aloud on television, I remember saying at one point, "Well, Dan, maybe we shouldn't get into that." But, of course, we did, and a whole lot more.

A year later, I still find it the strangest story I ever covered, strange because in all the other stories I've covered, I usually found someone to admire. In this one I became acquainted with an odd assortment of hypocrites, eccentrics, hustlers and tarts. But it was hard to find a hero. And I'll be frank: a year later, I still don't know exactly what to make of it. But I do know this much. It diminished everyone and everything it touched—the presidency, the Congress, the legal profession, politics, manners and, yes, the media.

Reporters love a good story, but I hope you won't take away my press pass when I tell you I hope we don't run across another one like this anytime soon.

—September 12, 1999

The Bush years would bring other kinds of scandal: bribery, outright lies to cover up the deaths of soldiers, cash payments to friendly journalists, sleazy attempts to slander political enemies. But it would be a while before we learned of those events. What worried me in the beginning when the debate over stem cells occurred was whether we had elected an administration that feared the future.

History-Makers Climb Mountains

History's longest argument has been over what to do about the mountain. One group has always wanted to cross the mountain, to explore and see what is on the other side.

The other group, no less sincere, has been willing to let well enough alone. They worry there might be things on the other side of the mountain we don't want to know.

They were the ones who refused to look through Galileo's telescope. They already knew all they needed to know about the moon and sun and stars.

Some will argue that the debate over stem cell research is more complicated than that.

But there is no argument about what history teaches. The store of knowledge increases when one generation is free to explore and build on what the previous generation has learned.

The ancient Chinese invented gunpowder and set it afire to ward off evil spirits. But the next generation harnessed its explosive power in a container and created the cannon. Later generations built on that and produced the internal combustion engine.

Science tells us the next step in stem cell research may yield cures for crippling diseases and ease the pain and suffering of millions.

Are we not obligated to see what is on the other side of this mountain?

History argues yes. The president says it is the hardest decision he will ever make.

But if he reads history, he will know that history remembers those who climbed the mountain, not those who stayed home in fear of the unknown.

—August 5, 2001

Every administration I have covered has come to office
telling us that presidents never rest.

Vacations

With President Bush heading off to his Texas ranch for the rest of the month, his handlers delivered the obligatory message, "This is not a vacation, it is a working vacation, because the president will be working."

All presidential staffers, no matter who is president, believe it is their constitutional responsibility to deliver that message and that the rest of us will actually believe it, which, of course, no one ever does.

I remember President Ford's aides explaining all this at the very moment the president was two hundred yards away, skiing down Vail mountain. When we asked the president later if he had come to Colorado to work, he laughed and said, "I come out here to ski. I've always come out here to ski."

Usually the handlers, though, are just following presidential orders. There is a memo in the National Archives in which President Nixon gives detailed and explicit orders to aides to explain that he never played one round of golf during a trip to California, as he put it, and this is a direct quote, "to build up points that this should not be charged as a vacation."

Was he worried we would dock his pay?

And remember how Bill Clinton ran polls to gauge voter reaction to his vacations? Is it better politics to go to the mountains or the beach? Now, there's an issue facing the nation.

Well, here is my take on all this. Everyone deserves a vacation, and my guess is most people don't begrudge any president, including this one, a little time off. And rest assured, the president will be working. Anyone who goes to central Texas in August has to work just to stay cool. I know, I grew up around there.

—*August 4, 2002*

Two presidents died during George Bush's presidency.
Here are three essays their deaths provoked.

Reagan's Wit and Optimism

Americans are by nature an optimistic people. Who but the optimistic would have crossed the Atlantic Ocean to found those first colonies? Or launched the American Revolution with the belief that it had any chance of success? Or headed west in covered wagons, unsure of where they were going or what they would find there?

Ronald Reagan with his cheerful attitude reflected that optimism. His critics poked fun at him. But he disarmed them by poking fun at himself.

When he was accused of being distracted, he told visitors to the Oval Office that "someday they will say Ronald Reagan slept here."

People loved him for it. You could hate his policies, but it was hard not to like him.

Critics underestimated him because he had started as an actor, but he always said his acting background helped him to communicate. He understood that communication is more than words. He had great respect for the presidency and that was reflected in the way he walked and talked. You never saw a bad picture of Ronald Reagan. By his demeanor, the American people sensed that he also had great respect and confidence in them, and perhaps that was the real reason for his popularity.

And he always found reason for hope. Even on that day when he announced in a handwritten letter to the American people that he had Alzheimer's, he reassured the country that as he began what he called the "journey that will lead me into the sunset of my life, I know that for America there will always be a bright dawn ahead."

Ronald Reagan always had an actor's sense of timing. He knew when it was time to leave the stage. And so it is fitting that he leaves this life at the time when world leaders will be in this country for the Economic Summit, which will make it convenient for them to attend his funeral.

I don't know what Ronald Reagan would have said about that, but I think he would have said something that would have made us smile.

—June 6, 2004

Lessons from Ronald Reagan

We spent all week thinking about Ronald Reagan, and that was a good thing. He was our president for eight years. He helped restore our national confidence when it was fading. When he left Washington, we didn't understand that the Soviet Union was so near collapse. Now we can see how the policy he put in place helped to bring down an enemy that for nearly half a century had the means to destroy us and all civilization. Reason enough to remember him.

But there is one more thing to think about. This week of tribute to Ronald Reagan was a refreshing respite in a presidential campaign that began too soon and has grown increasingly bitter when the country is already more polarized than ever. What Reagan showed us, what today's politicians would do well to remember, is that it is possible to have differences without hating those on the other side; that winning an argument does not have to mean destroying your opponent. Somehow that's been lost in today's mean politics. Years of negative campaigns conducted almost exclusively by thirty-second television ads have gridlocked our political process and made the compromises necessary to govern all but impossible. Worse, it has soured our politics to the point that too many people no longer want anything to do with it.

The lesson from Ronald Reagan is that his way did work. If our politicians would remember only that about him, the level of our political dialogue would rise and campaigns would again become interesting, perhaps even relevant to solving the problems of our times.

—June 13, 2004

My Favorite Presidential Interview

I have interviewed all the men who have served as president since Richard Nixon, and when I interviewed President Bush the other day, people asked what they always do: "Which was your favorite interview?"

They were surprised—and this is no reflection on any of the others—but I still have to say my very first presidential encounter.

It was 1969, Nixon had just come to office, and I was a rookie reporter in the CBS News Washington Bureau covering such prestigious assignments as the birth of the Washington Zoo's new tiger cub and the National Miniature Golf Championship.

I had just signed that one off when my mother called and demanded to know when I was "going to cover some real news." I explained I was not yet allowed to make my own assignments, but to my relief—my mother was a formidable woman—I was sent the next Sunday morning to cover a White House reception for the president's supporters.

It was such a minor affair that Helen Thomas of UPI and I were the only reporters there. A receiving line was set up, and when no one told us to stop, Helen and I just got in the line.

There was a story going round that the president was bringing in new advisers, and when it came my turn to shake his hand, I said,

"Mr. President, will these be outside people or in-house advisers?"

"Oh no," he said, "these will be outhouse advisers," and then real-izing what he had said, added, "Uh, well, you know what I mean," and wandered off into the crowd.

Not many would even call that an interview, and we did no story about it. But when I told my mother, she thought it was a great question.

—February 5, 2006

Ford's Clumsiness

Gerald Ford was an athlete in his youth, took care of himself all his life and was in great shape when he came to the White House.

Yet after he took a tumble or two on the ski slopes and then slipped one rainy day and fell headlong down the stairs coming off

Air Force One, he developed the reputation for clumsiness. The joke was Vice President Rockefeller was just a banana peel from the presidency.

It was completely unfair, but partly my fault, because I wrote a lot of those stories, but as someone said, "What are you gonna do if the president takes a header? Keep it a secret?"

The stories were great sight gags, but during the 1976 campaign I learned the hard way that the gods have a way of getting even with those who tell the same joke too many times.

When Mr. Ford stumbled, missed the door and bumped his head after a speech from the rear platform of a train in Kalamazoo, Michigan, I filed the obligatory story.

I thought it was hilarious, but afterward, as I rushed to catch a plane for the next campaign stop, it didn't seem quite so funny. As I was boarding the plane, someone hollered at me and, momentarily distracted, I walked head-on into the overhead luggage rack, brained myself and for an instant saw stars and passed out.

I wasn't really hurt, but the next time I saw the president, it seemed only fair to tell him about it. He laughed out loud and said, "By God, I just wish I could have been there to see it."

I think he meant it, too.

—*December 31, 2006*

*There are no schools and no experience that can fully
prepare anyone for the presidency, but this remains
one of the best guides I ever saw.*

"If I Were President"

Finally today, I call your attention to the words of eighteen-year-old Emily Nemeyer of Tampa, Florida. She recently won a contest sponsored by a student group called Freedom's Answer, in which teenagers were asked to complete the sentence "If I were president..." Her answer was published in today's *Parade* magazine, and here is what she wrote.

> *If I were president, I would remember what it was like to live with two hardworking parents barely eking out a living day by day. I would remember that there are always two, maybe even seven, sides to an argument. I would remember in times of war to visit the Vietnam Veterans Memorial to ponder if it is truly worth the price to inscribe that many names on a wall once more. I would remember what it's like to stand on a beach, staring at the ocean and feeling completely insignificant in the grand scheme of things. I would remember how it felt to watch the second tower collapse live on television. I would remember and swell with pride at being an American.*

The words of eighteen-year-old Emily Nemeyer. When she is old enough to run for president, she'll get my vote. She may even get it before then.

—March 14, 2004

V

LIFE, LIBERTY
AND THE PURSUIT
OF NEWS

W hen reporters and the academics who study journalism gather to talk about our craft, what they usually focus on is the impact that modern technology is having on what we do, and the changes have been astonishing.

The changes are no more remarkable than the speed at which they happened.

Younger reporters give me a double take when I remind them there was no television when I was young. I never saw a television set until I was in the eighth grade. Yet in less than my lifetime, technology made it possible for television to replace newspapers as the place where most people got their news, and now technology and the Internet are causing us to wonder if newspapers and print will even survive.

Hardly a day passes that I am not reminded of just how fast it has all happened. When my friend Susan Zirinsky, the CBS producer, gave me a portable typewriter like the ones we used to carry on political campaigns, Michelle Levi, my crack researcher and assistant at the time, admitted she had never seen one. By the time she was born, computer laptops had replaced portable typewriters. When I called Susan to thank her, I discovered her assistant had never seen one, either. And none of my younger colleagues seem to understand what it was like to be a reporter before cell phones, when finding a place to call it in was as important as finding the story.

The advances in telephone technology really and literally came home to me the day one of my granddaughters asked my wife why all the phones at our house had cords.

My wife explained that all phones once had cords, which brought this response:

"How did that work in cars?"

No one in or out of journalism can be less than awed with how much better the tools of our trade have become.

What we sometimes fail to notice is that the sophistication with which information is managed has changed almost as much as its technology, and just as rapidly, if not always for the better.

When I arrived in Washington in 1969, many members of Congress didn't have press secretaries. Now the most obscure member has a press secretary, consults with public relations specialists and sometimes retains a media coach. The basics of news management have become common practice in all aspects of American life, not just politics—everything from sartorial tips for what looks best on television to talking points, staying on message, giving the answer you want to give regardless of the question asked.

In Washington, every administration learns from the previous one and the lesson usually produces more secrecy. In his biography of the legendary New York Times *columnist James Reston, author John Stacks concludes that government officials of Reston's day felt some obligation to explain their actions, if only by doing it through anonymous leaks to senior pundits who explained it for them. He wondered if modern officials still felt that obligation. I'm not so sure they do, and have come to question whether the sophisticated spin we hear today may be redefining what we accept as truth. Is it truthful to reveal only part of the story when we know there are other parts that should be told? Is it ethical to reveal one thing while on the public payroll and tell an entirely different tale on leaving office?*

If journalism is to remain relevant, the answer to such questions may be as important as whether the iPod will someday replace newspapers. Technology has not changed the purpose of journalism, which remains to find the truth. Nor has it reduced the temptations of others to use it for their own and different purposes.

Finding the truth still depends more on the courage and the integrity of the individual journalist than it ever did on technology.

Journalism's product will always be more important than its tools.

Reporters were grappling with anonymous sources long before I came to Washington. What had once been an occasional way for officials to explain some action of the government that couldn't have been explained on the record for legitimate reasons (offending a foreign government, for example) became an art form in the hands of its most adroit practitioner, Henry Kissinger, who had come to Washington as Richard Nixon's first national security adviser. In 1974, the mass backgrounder had become a far-too-frequent part of Washington journalism. Four dozen reporters would be called into a room and told they couldn't quote the person doing the briefing. When told during one session we could identify the briefer only as "a senior American official," I made one "spokesman" furious when I asked if he would mind being identified as "a junior American official." A few days later, I resorted to the needle and wrote the follow-ing essay for CBS Radio. It did no good either, but I was pleased when, to my surprise, it showed up on the op-ed page of the Washington Post. *It had been put there by the paper's diplomatic correspondent Marilyn Berger, who said she hoped I didn't mind, and of course I didn't. I was delighted.*

The Senior American
Official

———

G uess who's in Germany taking a few days to relax and watch the
soccer matches—why, Senior American Official, that's who.

You remember him, of course. He's the anonymous fellow who
often shows up in various parts of the world where Henry Kissinger
happens to be visiting.

No one knows his name, but we do know several things for sure.
He apparently has wide contacts throughout the American press
establishment, because when he calls a news conference, all the
important reporters show up, and one thing is absolutely certain:
Senior American Official knows a lot about U.S. foreign policy.

It comes as no surprise, then, that Senior American Official is in
Germany this week, since Kissinger is also there. Kissinger isn't talking while he's in Germany. He's taking a few days' rest, but Senior
American Official is talking. In fact, Senior had a long conversation
yesterday with Murray Marder of the *Washington Post*.

According to Marder's story, Senior American Official gave an
assessment of the Moscow summit developments just a few hours
after Kissinger and his party flew into Düsseldorf from Moscow.

In his Düsseldorf interview, Senior American Official told Marder,
and we quote, "It is no mean accomplishment to hold the course of
detente under the conditions that exist in the United States."

What Senior was talking about, of course, was President Nixon.
He was also talking about the Watergate scandal, the threat of
impeachment and the effect of all that on the negotiations.

As Marder wrote it, this threat was inextricably entwined in the negotiating strategy on both sides, although both would deny it. No American president has ever engaged in high-stakes international diplomacy under such a cloud.

It was quite an interview, and just another indication of how far Senior has come since he joined the administration.

In the early days, Senior American Official's main responsibility was to brief newsmen on presidential foreign policy speeches. Henry Kissinger handled a lot of that later on, but, in the early days, White House image-makers were ashamed of Kissinger's German accent. They thought it would remind everyone of Doctor Strangelove, so the job of briefing the press on foreign policy fell to Senior American Official.

In those days, he usually went by the name Senior White House Official. It was not until Kissinger came out of the closet that Senior added the word "American" to his title.

As Kissinger began to travel, it was only natural that Senior American Official would go along, since he had acquired so many friends in the press through his White House briefing job. Since then, his life has been a veritable whirlwind—Vietnam, Paris, Peking, Moscow, the Middle East, Moscow again and now Düsseldorf.

It's been an exciting time for Senior American Official, and some say he's become quite a swinger in between press briefings. He's made a friend, or two, along the way—guys like Not For Attribution and Deep Background.

But it hasn't been easy, and Senior has collected a few enemies, too, the formidable Pentagon Source, for one.

Pentagon Source never did like Senior. They fell out early on, when Senior tried to blame a lot of the Vietnam dirty stuff on then Secretary of Defense Melvin R. Laird.

Lately, Pentagon Source has been furious because Kissinger and Senior American Official have joined Not For Attribution in inferring that the military's lack of restraint had something to do with the failure to get an arms agreement in Moscow.

In view of all this tension, we don't blame Senior American Official for taking a few days' rest in Germany. All of these fellows could use a vacation. Hopefully, they'll be able to find a nice, quiet spot where no one will recognize them and where they can get some real relaxation.

—July 5, 1974

Not every tradition in journalism is necessarily a good one. I am proud to say that stories about people who reach their hundredth birthday don't get in the paper nearly as often as they used to.

One-Hundred-Year-Old Man

One of the oldest traditions in journalism is the interview with the one-hundred-year-old man; for almost as long as there have been newspapers in this country, newspaper editors have been sending young reporters out to interview someone in the community who's just turned a hundred.

The interviews can usually be divided into two parts: (a) a discussion of how it feels to be a hundred years old, and (b) to what does the subject attribute reaching the age of a hundred. My favorite answer to (a) was given by the old man who said, "How do you think it would feel to be a hundred?"

The answer to (b), the secret of old age, usually has something to do with the interviewee's habit of smoking a big cigar and having a shot of whisky, or at least a glass of beer, every day; or, as seems the case in at least 50 percent of such interviews, not smoking a big cigar and refraining from having a shot of whisky, or at least a glass of beer, every day.

There have been so many interviews with one-hundred-year-old men, it is no wonder they are sometimes repetitive. After all, how much is there to say on the subject?

Well, be that as it may, here we go again, the *Washington Star,* one of the capital city's oldest institutions, has a new feature on its front pages these days called "Q & A." It's a daily interview with some prominent person or someone who might have something interesting to say, and wouldn't you know it, the interviewee in Sunday's paper was the area's most prominent senior citizen, Zachariah Blackestone, who is not just one hundred: Blackestone, a Washington florist, is 104.

Perhaps it was because he is 104 and has been through these interviews before, or perhaps it was just the skill of the interviewer, Louise Lague, but whatever the case, there was a new angle this time.

As Blackestone explained it, being 104 is about as you'd expect it to be—there are few surprises.

Blackestone said he had no particular advice to offer on how to live a long life; he said he doesn't do any special exercises, except to run up and down the hall a little after he wakes up in the morning.

And he attaches no special importance to drinking whisky or not drinking whisky.

The facts are, he said, he used to drink, but he doesn't anymore, since he found that as he grew older he became intoxicated more quickly. As Blackestone told it, the reason he's still around is because he's just continued to hang in there, and he said as far as he could tell, being 104 is not much different from being 103. Did he ever think he'd get there? Not really, it was like going from ninety-five to ninety-six. "I just came up to it," he said, "and after a while I was there." He said he always remembers what a friend told him when he was ninety-five: "Blacky," the friend said, "the one consolation is not many people die at age ninety-five." Blackestone also confirmed what most of us have suspected—when you're that age, you take most things in stride—you get the feeling you've seen it all before and it's hard to find friends your own age.

And he pointed out there are also some advantages: when someone wants to have him over for dinner, they know they'll have to come and get him and take him home when dinner's over; they realize that a man who's 104 years old can't be going out alone at night, driving an automobile.

Well, I don't know about you, but in this age when it's getting harder and harder to get a straight answer on anything, that kind of straight talk is downright soothing.

I hope the *Star* interviews Mr. Blackestone once a week, or better still, lets him write a column himself when he feels like it.

—*March 10, 1975*

We thought back in 1996 that the conventions
were becoming infomercials. We had
no idea what was to come.

Kicking the Tires

———

S ince the GOP convention and over the last couple of days, at
least two dozen people have stopped me and asked where I
stand on this question of whether the networks were used by the
Republicans and whether we should devote so much time and effort
to an event that produced so little news.

The answer to both questions is yes. It's nothing new for journalists
to be used. Franklin Roosevelt used us when he asked for free airtime
to tell America about Pearl Harbor. But that was right, not wrong.

As for the conventions, we should first understand what they've
become. With the nominating done long before they even begin, they
become more akin to an auto show than old-time politics. When the
automakers roll out a new model, they display it in the best possible
setting. It's their car and they're welcome to show it off any way they
please. That's as it should be. The auto press looks it over, maybe
kicks the tires, and then writes what they please. Sometimes the
company likes it; sometimes it doesn't. That's as it should be.

It may be easy news to get, but people want to know what the new
model looks like and what to expect of it. Well, it's much the same
with modern conventions. The parties show off their candidates any
way they please. We look them over, write what we please, and that,
too, for the same reasons, is how it ought to be.

There are some questions for both sides. Can the parties really get their message out if there's so little news they risk putting people to sleep? And should we spend millions of dollars and send hundreds of people to cover an event that promises so few surprises?

I'm one who believes journalists' first responsibility is to show up just in case news happens, but we probably don't need to send so many people and spend so much as we did in the days when we had no idea what might happen.

—August 18, 1996

On February 21, 2002, I was to be given a lifetime achievement award by the National Press Foundation at a huge dinner in Washington. I had planned to talk about the First Amendment in my acceptance speech, but just hours before the dinner news broke that Daniel Pearl, a young reporter for the Wall Street Journal, *had been brutally killed by terrorists. I set aside what I had planned to say and wrote the following.*

For Danny Pearl, Who Tried to Get It Right

D anny Pearl. I never met him but I knew him because I was a young reporter once.

What I learned when I went to Vietnam a long time ago is that there are two kinds of people who show up at wars. There are the thrill seekers who have nothing to lose and for them it is the ultimate hunting trip—where the animals shoot back.

They are not brave, they are the foolhardy.

And then there are those who recognize the danger, who have so much to lose and yet they go on. They are the ones with courage.

Danny Pearl was one of those. And that is why we are so proud of him. Because he did what journalists are supposed to do. He went to where the story was. He didn't have to go but he went because he wanted to get the story right.

Getting it right is what we are supposed to do. That is not a complicated thing but it can be a dangerous thing. And it can be a noble thing.

In this age of instant, easy communications, when we are literally bombarded by news from all sides, too often we take for granted how difficult and dangerous it is to gather the news.

We confuse television scenes with reality. Even some of us on television do that. Television brings the battlefield into the living room and we see so much that danger becomes routine. Just another TV show. You don't get the blood on you watching a war on television.

And then somebody kills a kid like Danny Pearl and we are brought back to reality, back to the world where bullets kill and those who die leave behind pregnant wives.

September 11 and all that has come after it has not been an easy story for any of us because we have been a part of it.

We have been trained to believe that we are at our best when we can report dispassionately, when we can put distance between ourselves and those we cover.

But we couldn't do it on this one.

On the morning of the attack I was headed for the Capitol, where I usually spend my day.

Perhaps I owe my life to those brave passengers who forced down the plane in Pennsylvania, because we now believe that plane was headed to where I would have been that day.

I couldn't forget that as I reported this story. Nor will I ever forget those passengers who forced that plane down.

On the Friday before the attack my own brother had spent six hours in the very area of the Pentagon where that plane hit it on Tuesday. Had the attack come on Friday, he might well have died.

I could never forget that. Nor could I forget the anthrax and the Cipro and the anxiety that came with that.

But I am not unique. Each of us in this room has a similar story. Everyone knows someone who had a close call or someone who died. And now all of us know about Danny Pearl.

These are times when all of us have been reminded that no matter what our profession, journalist, plumber, fireman, public official or accountant, we are all Americans. We are all in this together.

But it is during this awful time, as we have come to recognize our vulnerability, that I believe we have come to be more aware of those around us and more appreciative of the part that each of us plays to make our Democracy work.

And so we didn't stop reporting on September 11. We went on and covered the story just as we will go on and cover the story tomorrow because that is our part and our responsibility.

I was so struck tonight to hear the reporters and editors of the *Wall Street Journal* say that in the hours after September 11 as they decided how to respond, they decided that what they knew how to do was put out a newspaper—and so that is what they did.

The historian Ariel Durant once said that "Barbarism, like the jungle, does not die out but only retreats behind the barriers that civilization has thrown up against it, and waits there always to reclaim that to which civilization has temporarily laid claim."

More than ever we have come to understand that since September 11.

But what we also know is that *knowledge* and *information* are the barriers that civilization throws up against barbarism.

We marvel at the miracles of technology, but what we as journalists must always remember is that the power we have is in the words, not the technology we use to transmit them.

By television standards the ancient Greeks didn't get very high ratings. Their audiences on the hillsides of Athens seldom numbered more than a dozen. Yet their words and the words of Jesus and Moses and yes, Muhammad, traveled around the world many times long before there were satellites or even a Xerox machine.

It is the transmission of knowledge, the eradication of ignorance that is civilization's great and only real defense against barbarism.

And it is the only real reason for what we have come to call journalism. But it is reason enough.

That is why people like Danny Pearl go on in the face of danger. They go on to get it right. To get the truth.

So I thank you for tonight. It is a sad night but I thank you for your friendship and for the recognition you have given to me and for this time together.

And I say to you, be proud of your country and be proud of a profession that has included so many like young Danny Pearl who had the courage to go wherever they needed to go to get the story right.

Remember him and all those who came before him and be proud of what you do.

—February 21, 2002

*Modern communications also remind us we have
plenty not to be proud of.*

Escapism at the
Paris Hilton

E ver since I read that more people watched Paris Hilton's reality
TV show than watched Diane Sawyer's interview with George
Bush after the capture of Saddam Hussein, it has really bothered
me. Part of the problem for me was I didn't know at the time who
Paris Hilton was, but still, I thought, there has got to be some reason.
Maybe, I thought, in this age when political spin rules, we no longer
expect our politicians to tell us much, so we just tune all of them out.

But then I reread one of William Manchester's books about
Churchill, and then I decided the answer may go beyond that.
Because Manchester said that World War I was the first historical
event where reality outstripped imagination. What he meant was
that the carnage was so horrible, no one could have imagined it, and
afterward it produced such revulsion to war that Europe's people
were plunged into denial that ran so deep they were unable to see
there was something worse coming.

Churchill tried to warn them, but his people ignored him and
instead they were transfixed by stories in the British press about
the adventures of the vicar of Steedham, who had amazing success seducing waitresses, was found out, defrocked and began a new
career taming lions, only to be eaten by one. It was all people could
talk about.

Has Paris Hilton become our vicar of Steedham?

Was the horror of 9/11 so beyond our imagination that we've tried to escape into the unreality and vulgarity of reality television, rather than coming to grips with the fact that there is far worse ahead if we do not eradicate terrorism? Terrorism is not reality television. It is reality, the reality we have a choice to face or avoid as we begin another year.

—January 12, 2004

No Bribe Left Behind

News that the Department of Education paid talk show host Armstrong Williams what amounts to a $240,000 bribe to promote its No Child Left Behind legislation is so outrageous it borders on laughable.

Except I'm not amused when the government uses my money—tax dollars—to try to con *me*.

Every large organization, including CBS, has a few stupid people, and on occasion they do stupid things. But what I don't understand is why all this caused hardly a ripple at the White House.

The only response from there that I could find in yesterday's papers was that a spokesman referred all questions to the Department of Education.

Why go there for answers, where the whole loony idea originated? The same department that had earlier spent some $700,000 to survey which reporters favored No Child Left Behind and which opposed it?

I can't imagine that the president or anyone else with half a brain thought this was a good idea. But wouldn't you think the White House would want us to know that? Has the administration become so convinced of its own righteousness that it refuses to denounce even this sort of thing? Did they think we wouldn't notice?

Forget the details. Trying to corrupt the news media with bribes is wrong. If the Department of Education people haven't figured that out, then the president should educate them. A good lesson plan might include firing those responsible.

Then he should promise the rest of us that it will never happen again.

—*January 9, 2003*

The part that does make me proud.

Getting the Story

I get a lot of mail about bias. I can't remember giving a lecture when I wasn't asked about it.

If my mail is a measure, many conservatives believe most reporters are Democrats driven by a liberal bias. Many liberals believe reporters are so cowed by the Bush administration that we go too easy on Republicans.

My standard answer is that yes, some reporters *are* biased—not many, but a few. Like a draft army, the press reflects the society from which it is drawn and contains many points of view.

But I argue that what drives the vast majority of reporters is not a hidden political agenda, but a desire to get the story and to get it before their competitors.

I never heard that better explained than last week at the opening of the Watergate papers of Bob Woodward and Carl Bernstein, which have been placed at the University of Texas. The notes, transcripts, the raw data compiled by these two great reporters are a trove of information for scholars.

But the trip to Austin was worth it just to hear Woodward describe what motivated them as they delved into the minor burglary that eventually brought down a president. They had no hidden agenda, nor any idea how the story would end.

Woodward said, "We were just trying to find out what happened."

In those few words, he summed up journalism's whole purpose, and they should be posted above the door of every newsroom in America— the last thing reporters see as they head out on assignment.

When we forget them and try to overly complicate our purpose, we get into trouble. When we remember them, we can perform a valuable, even noble service.

I still believe that is what most reporters do.

—February 6, 2005

Practicing What We Preach in Iraq

When I read those stories about the military secretly paying Iraqi journalists and their newspapers to print American propaganda, it made me think of a man named Garrett Morris.

Garrett is well into his eighties now, and his name won't mean anything to you unless you're from Fort Worth, Texas, but he is one of the wisest men I've ever known.

Thirty-three years ago, my younger brother, all of twenty-four years old and still in graduate school, decided to run for a seat in the Texas State Legislature. He was an underdog, and a friend suggested a real dirty trick to use on his opponent.

He went to Garrett for advice, and I'll never forget Garrett's answer: "Never do something in a campaign that you'll be ashamed of if you're found out, and besides that wouldn't be effective."

So why in the world, when we are trying to convince the Iraqis of the strength and efficacy of democratic institutions, would we try to do it by corrupting their press, one cornerstone of democracy? The government writes the stories for a totalitarian press, not a democracy's press.

This administration has never had much use for reporters, and that is their privilege. But speeches about democratic values ring hollow when the speechmaker gets caught trying to undermine democratic institutions.

We can do better than that. If this is a war over values, we can best demonstrate the strength of our values by practicing them. To do otherwise, after all, is just not effective.

My brother, by the way, took Garrett's advice. He was elected that year and two times after.

—December 4, 2005

*Garrett Morris died in 2007, but in the last weeks of
his life people still looked to him for advice.*

Every so often...

Sometimes, Good Things Happen

S omeone asked me the other day if it bothered me to announce bad news.

The flip answer would be, "I guess not, or I would have found another job a long time ago."

Because the truth is, most of what we report is bad news.

When there's a fire down the street from your house, that isn't welcome news, but you sure want to know about it, and we see it as our job to tell you.

Still, there is so much bad news that I sometimes think we ought to start our newscast by saying, "I hate to be the one to tell you this but..."

Not so last week, when Warren Buffett said he would turn over $31 billion to Bill Gates's foundation and let Gates decide how to give it away.

It made me feel good just to announce it. What an example to all of us.

So many channel their charitable giving to reflect maximum credit on themselves, but Buffett followed the rule he has followed in business: get good people to run your operation and then stay out of their way.

On charity, the Bible speaks of doing it so secretly that even the left hand won't know what the right hand is doing. Buffett went one better, keeping both hands off and letting Gates do it. "He'll have a clearer head six feet above ground than I will six feet under," he said.

I hope there'll be more news like that, but the world being what it is, it will probably be a while.

—*July 2, 2006*

Read all about it!

A Case for Newspapers

With iPods and blogs and the Internet, there is a lot of serious talk about whether newspapers will survive. But the awful news of last week reminded me just how much we need them, and not always for the obvious reasons.

Jill Abramson, who is the managing editor of the *New York Times*, says we use the Internet to search for specific information. But the joy of reading a newspaper comes from finding information we weren't looking for.

Last week reminded me of that. The main news was so grim I found myself turning to the newspapers for relief.

Deep in the *Times* one day last week, surrounded by all the war news, I found an obituary of Robert Brooks, who founded the Hooters restaurant chain. The writer said Hooters was known for spicy chicken wings and even spicier waitresses. Who could read that and not at least smile?

I found another story about the death of Arthur Haggerty. I

learned he was credited with making dog-training into a respectable profession, and was known to legions of dogs as "he who must be obeyed." Hadn't known of him myself, but I won't forget him after reading that.

And then there was the story I found on the business page that began: "Robie Livingstone has all but given up on having a positive underwear-buying experience."

How can you *not* read on when a story starts that way?

Maybe it's just me, but I was in a better humor after reading those stories.

Of course it didn't last long, as the day wore on and the rest of the news rolled in.

—July 23, 2006

The best thing I never did.

We Didn't Get the Paris Interview

I have let you down, and I think it's best to just admit it and move on. *Face the Nation* did not get the big interview with Paris Hilton.

I feel terrible about it.

I haven't felt so low since one of our competitors broke into programming to report that the embalming of Anna Nicole Smith's body had begun. Getting scooped on a big story is never fun, not then, not ever. And we never got to first base on that story, either, which is why we tried to be competitive on this one.

We held strategy sessions on how to stay ahead on the Paris story. In the finest network tradition, we blamed each other for not getting the interview. We even leaked the infighting to competitors. But nothing worked.

All those big-time bookers dangled all those deals in front of Paris's family, and we were just out of our league. Heck, we couldn't even figure out what league we were in.

As Paris herself might've summed it up, "Whatever."

When the deals for the other networks fell through, my friend Larry King got the interview, and to show what a big deal that is, this morning the *New York Times* took note of it on page one.

There's nothing left for me to do but stop making excuses and fess up.

The truth is, I never asked Paris Hilton to be on *Face the Nation*, and for one reason: I couldn't think of anything I wanted to ask her. Can you?

—*June 24, 2007*

VI

WAR AND PEACE

W hen George Bush sent American troops into Iraq because he believed Saddam Hussein had weapons of mass destruction, I thought he had no choice and said so.

Only two years earlier, we had been blindsided by 9/11. Saddam was a brutal dictator who had used poison gas on his own people and later killed the husbands of his own daughters. That kind of person was capable of anything, I thought, and if he had a nuclear weapon, it was only a matter of time until he used it.

But we got it wrong.

American troops went to Iraq and toppled Saddam, but they found no such weapons. Colin Powell's recall of the Pottery Barn warning "If you break it, you own it" became tragically true. (Actually, it was New York Times columnist Tom Friedman who coined the phrase.)

We may have invaded Iraq with the best of intentions, but we went there on the basis of bad intelligence and a plan of attack that was even worse.

American officials were so convinced of what they intuitively believed, they sold themselves a bill of goods—they saw what they wanted to see in the intelligence estimates and somehow disregarded the things that argued against their core convictions.

Defense Secretary Rumsfeld was in the midst of overhauling the military establishment. He was determined to prove that a small, fast-moving army could do the job that large, lumbering armies of the past had done—and do it better. He was wrong.

In March of 2003, American bombers pounded Iraq from above,

and the invading American army quickly reached Baghdad. Saddam's elite forces fled as Saddam's statue was toppled in one of the capital's public squares. What we failed to notice was that not much had changed in the rest of the country as the invading troops raced by. Many in Saddam's army and the old dictator himself disappeared into the civilian population, many with their weapons.

The administration had expected our troops to be greeted as liberators; instead there was widespread looting, and the invading American force was too small to control it. Nor were there enough troops to guard the ammunition dumps that Saddam's army abandoned. Explosives from those unguarded stockpiles are still being used to kill American troops.

We freed the Iraqi people from the iron grip of one of history's worst tyrants, but with no real plan for what to do next, we left a power vacuum that led to chaos. When we disbanded the Iraqi army, we left them with no way to feed their families in a country where most of the infrastructure had been destroyed and there were no jobs.

Whether it would have been a different story had there been a better plan can only be conjectured, but I have come to believe the greater mistake was that we simply chose the wrong way and the wrong place to center our war on the growing threat of terrorism.

We toppled Saddam, and the world is a better place without him, but the danger posed by terrorism is as real as it ever was. That threat has changed our lives more than we sometimes realize. The instant some unexpected event occurs—a plane crash, a major fire or a natural disaster—our first reaction is, "Are terrorists responsible?" We endure the inconvenience of endless airport security lines. Hidden cameras monitor our every move in public places, and there is an ongoing debate over the government's right to challenge our privacy in the name of national security. We have come to accept and sometimes no longer notice how the beauty of Washington's majestic buildings and monuments has been marred by the sight of ugly but necessary barricades. Worse, we have come to realize we are embroiled in a war where Americans continue to die but where there are no longer any good answers.

Until the factions within Iraq's government come to a realistic, work-able agreement on how to share power, whatever gains American troops have made there will count for nothing. Yet no matter how long we keep our troops there, there is no guarantee the factions will come together. In truth, there is no real sign that they will. That Iraq can one day stand alone remains a goal, but is still a question not yet answered.

Even so, a sudden withdrawal of U.S. forces would surely leave a dangerous impression that we have either given up or have been defeated—an impression that would not only threaten the security of our allies in the region but the security of America as well.

Over the course of the long war since 9/11, I closed our Face the Nation *broadcast many times with reflections on the war. In the beginning, I was hopeful, but as the years passed, I came to temper my expectations about what America could and could not accomplish. As the conflict dragged on, I began to hear and see so many things I had heard before in those long-ago days when I had been a young reporter in Vietnam—the question, "Are we winning?" which was always the wrong question. Victory is always obvious; when we have to ask, we are losing. As it was during Vietnam, I began to see the progress reports, which never seemed to match the pictures we saw on television, and again we were bombarded with a blizzard of statistics that were never so much wrong as irrelevant.*

Vietnam and Watergate had torn America apart. The credibility of the government had been shattered and we had become distrustful of not only our national institutions but of each other. I was a child during World War II, and on the Sunday after 9/11, I wrote that the unprovoked attack had caused Americans to come together as they had not done since those days. I said that the attack had helped us to finally get past Vietnam. But the unity we felt in those weeks after 9/11 soon unraveled as the war went badly and there were no weapons of mass destruction. The administration struggled to justify the reasons for going to Iraq and overstated progress in an attempt to rally support.

Yet instead of coming together as I had thought, the country became more divided than it had been since Vietnam. As the collection of essays in this chapter shows, events often caused me to reflect not just on Vietnam, but on those childhood days of World War II.

Pitching In

I went to see the *Pearl Harbor* movie this weekend. I was four when that attack happened, so I don't remember that, but I was eight going on nine when the war finally ended, so I can remember a lot about it.

How we moved around because my dad was part of a team building a bomb factory, and then moving again when he got drafted, and then moving again when they didn't take him because the war was about over and they weren't taking men with children.

I remember going to four different schools in the first grade, and food and gasoline rationing, and neighbors who lost people in the war. All our lives were disrupted, but we all pitched in, even the kids. We all knew somebody in the army and what they were doing for us.

And that's the part that bothers me now. In this era of peace and the all-volunteer army, fewer and fewer of us have any connection to the military.

Many Americans no longer even know someone in the service. We need a movie to remind us that young Americans are still out there for us.

After I saw *Pearl Harbor*, I had the same thought I had after seeing *Saving Private Ryan*. Would Americans still do what those young Americans did? I don't know, but I want to believe we would.

As we left the movie, my wife said, "I'm glad we went. It helps me remember Memorial Day is more than the start of summer." Not a bad thought—not a bad thought to start every summer.

—May 27, 2001

A Death in the Family

I remember the day Franklin Roosevelt died.

I was riding on my mother's grocery cart at the grocery store. And when we got to the checkout counter, everybody was crying, and when my mother told me why, she began to cry, so I cried, too.

I can also remember the war years, when sugar and gasoline were rationed and we ate margarine because there was no butter.

And I remember moving back and forth to my grandmother's house as we waited for my dad to be drafted.

It turned our lives upside down, but I can't ever remember my parents talking about doing something heroic. It was just something that had to be done, and we were all in it together, and so they did it.

I guess that's why I've never been very comfortable with the administration's admonition that the best way to fight the terrorists is to go shopping. I understand this logic, but there wasn't much to buy in World War II.

It was a shared sacrifice of making do with very little that got us through that.

So I will do my duty this Christmas season and go shopping, but I will also remember Pearl Harbor and my father and mother and how they endured; first, because I love them, but also because it helps me to understand what we are really capable of as a people when we all work together.

If we should ever forget what they did, we will risk forgetting what we can do. And only then will the terrorists win.

Remember Pearl Harbor.

—December 9, 2001

Our Policy and Our Aim

I have been reading a lot about World War II lately, so maybe that's why I thought of Winston Churchill the other day when another terrorist scare surfaced and I heard someone on TV say, "That's just how it's going to be from now on."

No, I thought, that's just how it is right now. Yes, we all know that the inconveniences and precautions of today's world are necessary, taking off our shoes to board an airplane, barricades around the Capitol. But we must never resign ourselves to believing that it has to be that way forever.

In May of 1940, when most Americans wanted no part of the war in Europe, and most of Europe believed the Nazis were so powerful that there was no alternative but a continent dominated by Germany, and no choice but to appease Hitler, this is what Winston Churchill said: "You ask, 'What is our policy?' I will say it is to wage war. You ask, 'What is our aim?' I can answer in one word; victory at all cost; victory in spite of terror; victory, however long and hard the road may be; for without victory, there is no survival."

We can erect barricades and we can set up surveillance cameras and all the rest. But until we eradicate terrorism, our way of life cannot survive.

If that means reinstituting the draft, so be it.

If that means American troops posted in Iraq for as long as they were stationed in Germany, so be it.

If that means spending billions to attack the root causes of terrorism, it will be money well spent. The world we want for our children is the world we once knew, not the world of today. And we can promise them no less. Like Churchill, our aim must be victory.

—November 17, 2002

Service

The other night the president urged people who want to join the war on terrorism to join the Peace Corps and other volunteer organizations.

It is a great idea, but here's why I won't be elected president. I would ask Congress to pass a law making it mandatory that everyone at age eighteen be required to give one year of service to the country. Just a year, in the military or teaching or at a hospital or in the Peace Corps.

When I was coming up, we didn't have a choice. It was, be drafted into the army for two years or take ROTC in college and spend three years in the service as an officer.

I chose Air Force ROTC, not for noble reasons. Because it was a better deal, is why I chose it rather than two years as an army grunt.

But it was the best thing I ever did. I did things I never would have done, and I was thrown together with people from every corner and every walk of America.

I thought about that as I watched the Enron hotshots explain their financial expertise to Congress last week. They all went to the best schools. But I wondered if they might have been more sensitive to their workers if they had been exposed to the cross section of Americans they might have met in a draft army.

In ROTC we were taught that a leader's first responsibility is to his people. Were the Enron officers thinking of their people, the shareholders and the Enron workers? Did they even know any of the workers who lost their life's savings? Or did they follow the farmer's rule: don't name an animal you may have to eat?

We'll never see the draft again. But we need to find a way to bring young people from every stratum of America together.

The draft did that. It helped us to know each other and to know the pride that comes only when we feel we've been part of making something better. The draft forced those lessons on my generation.

I don't know if the country benefited from my small service, but I sure did.

—*February 10, 2002*

Ben Hua

It was thirty-four years ago, just about this time of the year, when I was a hotshot young reporter for the *Fort Worth Star-Telegram* and was two weeks away from completing an assignment in Vietnam.

Because my job had been to track down Texas kids and write stories about them, I'd spent most of my time in the field, but I didn't want to risk getting killed in those final days, so I stayed closer to headquarters, which is why I went one day to a military hospital at Ben Hua.

As it is when you're young, I had somehow come to believe that I was bulletproof, but as I was led into that amputee ward, I suddenly realized just how permanent the scars of war can be. The war had become controversial by then, but as I talked with those men—boys, really—who had lost arms and legs and hands and feet, I realized that no matter who proved to be right about whether we should be in Vietnam, those arms and legs would never grow back.

I was never quite as brave after that, but the war would prove a turning point in my life, because it led to my job here at CBS News.

I've never forgotten those young men who also went back to "the world," as they called it, not as nature made them, but as war left them. On this Memorial Day, we honor those who gave their lives for our country, but we should also remember so many who also gave so much.

—May 28, 2000

Bob Kerrey's Story

I went to Vietnam as a reporter in 1965. And the first thing I learned was that war is not as it was portrayed in those old World War II movies, where death was always noble, usually neat and bloodless, and everything went according to plan. In Vietnam, I discovered death was never neat, injuries were often gruesome and almost nothing went as planned. Accidents happened.

I thought of all that when I watched the furor explode around Bob Kerrey, the Congressional Medal of Honor winner, last week, who confessed to an awful and tragic mistake. Before he won that medal and before his foot was blown away by a hand grenade, his small group of men was fired on in the dark. He says they fired back, only to discover they had killed innocent women and children. The confession came as another member of his unit said the innocents were shot on purpose.

For the record, I choose to believe Kerrey, because I have known him to be an honorable person.

But there is a larger point here that goes beyond this episode.

It should remind us of the awful burden we place on young people when we send them into war where they not only risk their lives but find every value they hold is tested. We are humane people, but John McCain, whose credentials are pretty good in this area, said the other day that we send our people into combat with conflicting expectations. We expect them to be good people and we expect them to kill.

Only as a last resort, only when all else has failed, should we ever put our young people in such a position. War is no movie and there is little good to be said about it.

—April 29, 2001

An Uneasy Feeling

Too much of what happened last week reminded me of Vietnam.

When President Clinton went to the Pentagon to say he might have to bomb Iraq, it reminded me of how Lyndon Johnson always had to make his speeches on military bases to avoid being drowned out by protesters.

Maybe Clinton, the old war protester, sensed what the rest of us missed, because the next day his top Cabinet officers got an unmerciful heckling at an Ohio State campus when they tried to explain the rationale for bombing Iraq.

And then the next day, as the secretary of state told another group of students there was a difference between war and military action, I suddenly remembered how carefully government spokes-men chose their words during Vietnam, substituting phrases such as "collateral damage" for killing civilians.

The prevailing wisdom within the administration seems to be, "We ought to do something about Saddam," though no one seems quite sure just what. And as so often happened during Vietnam, for all its words, the administration seemed unable this week to say exactly what bombing would accomplish, except that if it didn't work, more bombing might be needed.

Let us just hope that today's news from Iraq, that a deal to avert war is in the making, proves true. If so, that would mean that the threat to bomb may have given Saddam second thoughts about con-tinuing to defy UN inspectors and we'll have avoided war for the moment.

But those of us who remember Vietnam have heard before that peace is at hand, so we suspect this won't be the end of it.

Saddam will still be there and there still seems to be no clear strategy of what can or should be done about it. How many times during Vietnam did we have that same uneasy feeling?

—February 22, 1998

This one looks pretty good in retrospect.

Duct Tape and Tax Cuts

W e must have a little disclosure. When the president first talked of cutting taxes, it was just fine by me.

To be absolutely selfish about it, I would benefit more than most from a tax cut. But that was before 9/11, and when the administration's tax plan was formally introduced last week, the whole thing seemed unreal to me.

Here we are about to go to war, but first we're going to cut taxes? I've never heard of a country that did that. And when the secretary of defense told Congress later in the week that it would be impossible to estimate the cost of a war if there is one, the idea of cutting taxes moved from unreal to the category of preposterous.

Now I'm no economist, but I think I do know something about communicating, and the most important message the administration is trying to drive home these days is that Saddam Hussein poses a grave threat that must be eliminated.

I happen to agree with that; others don't.

But the administration is hurting its case when it tells us in one breath that the threat of terrorism is so great we must all rush out and buy duct tape, then tells us later that we can go ahead and conduct business as usual and still defeat it, that getting rid of Saddam can be done so easily and cheaply that there's no need to postpone a tax cut that was designed long before Saddam was seen as such a threat.

That is not a mixed message. It's a message that simply does not add up. Nor, if we go to war, does it make much sense to leave the bill for our children.

We need to set some priorities here. First, defeat terrorism, then worry about a tax cut.

—March 2, 2003

Spinning out of control.

The Spin on War

The kindest way to put it is to say the White House got caught last week with its talking points down. All week, officials told reporters the president had not been keeping up with the war on television. That's standard practice in a political campaign. Image-makers never want us to believe their man keeps up with news coverage. Admit that and they have to admit he's aware of what the critics are saying, and they would have you believe he's above all that.

But now we know, courtesy of Elisabeth Bumiller of the *New York Times*, the president has been watching TV. One of the president's oldest friends told her the president, as any intelligent person would, checks television frequently to get war updates and that he laughed when he heard a reporter quote White House officials who said he didn't watch TV.

Now that's small stuff, but it's another indication that the government's official spokesmen, military and civilian, are too often putting out political spin instead of information.

I believe we had no choice but to disarm Saddam, but rallying public support, with all that spin in the beginning about how easy it would be, worried me from the start.

That's why it bothered me when the army's top ground commander in Iraq said the enemy was not reacting the way we expected, and official spokesmen dismissed his comments as if he were a campaign operative who had gotten off message.

One official spokesman even suggested the general didn't have the big picture. Excuse me? The top ground commander didn't have the big picture?

If the administration wants to be believed, and that will be necessary to hold public support, the message it needs to stay on is to forget the spin, acknowledge mistakes, stick to the truth, then get on with winning the war.

This is a war, not a campaign, and Americans know the difference.

—*March 30, 2002*

Two good men.

War Reporters

The technology is so good, the pictures are so clear, that it is sometimes difficult to separate the war from the other programs on television. We take the technology for granted, and that makes it easy to forget just how dangerous war is, that this is not a movie where the soldiers get up for a retake after being shot. And it is just as easy to forget the risks that people take to get those pictures from the battlefield to our living rooms. And then we're brought back to reality. Soldiers die, and so do the reporters telling their stories.

Last week, we learned of the death of Michael Kelly, the *Washington Post* columnist, who died when his vehicle overturned in a canal. He leaves a wife and two sons.

Today we learned of the death of NBC News correspondent David Bloom, a gentle man and as brave a reporter as I ever knew, who died from a blood clot in the lungs after pushing himself to the limit, and past it, as he traveled with American troops as they made their way to Baghdad. He leaves a wife and three daughters.

I knew both of them, and it was not the glamour of the job that drew them to the battlefield, but a passion to be where the story was, which is what reporters are supposed to do. Because they and the rest of the reporters covering the war have been there, the rest of us are getting a new appreciation of the job the American military has been doing, and because of those reporters, the propaganda from Saddam Hussein's people is put to the lie daily.

Let these reporters' deaths remind us that this is not a television show, an option for those who don't like basketball. This is a war. People die, and the loss and human suffering is borne most of all by the families of both those who fight the wars and the reporters who tell their stories.

—April 6, 2003

*If only it could have happened in the way
I hoped it could that day.*

What Comes Next

Watching our military crush Saddam has left me in awe, and my guess is most Americans feel the same way.

But as the smoke clears over Baghdad, here's the part that worries me: Are we emphasizing the right reasons for going to Iraq? I believe there was good reason for what we did. Saddam posed a grave threat to this country and had to be disarmed. But all this talk lately about how this may be part of a larger effort to remake that part of the world leaves me a little uneasy, mainly because it only fuels the hatred for us there. And make no mistake, it is real hatred.

Not many will miss the maniac Saddam, but there is always a natural resentment to powerful outsiders, and we are the ultimate powerful outsider. And there is resentment because some are convinced we came there for the oil, and as it always is, because some believe Israel is somehow behind all of this.

The way to counter this, it seems to me, is obvious: bring in as many nations as possible to help restore order and share in helping to rebuild Iraq. Then we must leave as quickly as we came.

That won't take away from our victory, but enhance it. We scored a spectacular success in Iraq, but real security will depend on what comes next.

If we want to take down the barricades and the metal detectors and stop undressing at the airport, we must rebuild our traditional alliances and convince the Arab world it has no reason to hate us.

Getting out of Iraq may be as important to our long-term security as going in was.

> —*April 13, 2003*

Going It Alone

The administration tells us we're in a worldwide war against terrorism. I believe that. But sometimes I wonder if the administration does.

Telling us, for example, to go shopping and get on with our lives after raising the terror threat level may be good, calming politics, but is that the best way to rally support in wartime? And now I read we may send a man back to the moon to improve morale?

A trip to the moon in the middle of a war? Surely not.

And if this is a world war, shouldn't we be bringing the rest of the world in to help us fight it? The greatest generation had far greater differences with the Soviet Union than the silly arguments over money that have estranged us from our European allies. Yet they found a way to work with the Soviets to defeat the Nazis.

Other countries refuse to put their troops into harm's way in Iraq because we won't let them have a say in what happens there. And while we argue with them over who gets to sell cement and phone service to the Iraqis, it is our troops that are taking the brunt of the casualties. Now where is the advantage in that?

We cannot remake the world in our image, but what we can do is work with the rest of the civilized world to create conditions that allow all people to find their own paths to freedom and liberty. Logic argues that cannot work unless the rest of the civilized nations join in the effort.

America was never afraid to lead in confronting the Nazis, or in rebuilding Europe and Japan after the war.

We led, but we were never foolish enough to believe we could do any of it alone.

—December 28, 2003

Honesty Still the Best Policy

Secretary of Defense Don Rumsfeld says one source of America's problems these days is that we are losing the public relations war to Al Qaeda.

In a speech to the Council on Foreign Relations, he said, "The U.S. government still functions as a five-and-dime store in an eBay world."

Boy, did he get that part right, but, man, is he wrong about why.

I've dealt with Brother Rumsfeld since he was President Ford's chief of staff and I like the guy. Not long ago I reminded him that "we've been arguing with each other for thirty years." We both laughed.

But here's where I believe he is wrong. He thinks the press makes too much of horrible events such as Abu Ghraib. I don't.

A democracy by definition means openness. The founding fathers knew enough about human nature to know government would always cover up its mistakes if it operated in secret. Bringing mistakes to the fore is a strength, not a weakness.

When America outlawed segregation, it acknowledged two hundred years of wrongs far worse than Abu Ghraib. Would anyone argue that publicly correcting those wrongs made us weaker? To the contrary, it made us stronger. It showed the world we live by the values we preach. And that those values work.

This administration has been secretive when there was no real point to it, has paid reporters to take the government line and has left the impression that bad news exists only in the minds of reporters. That's no way to win a PR war. It's a sure way to lose it.

Our strength comes from emphasizing in every word and action the values that separate us from those who oppose us, not from adopting their methods.

—February 19, 2006

"No Excuse, Sir"
Is the Only Answer

When I was in the Air Force—a long, long time ago—I was told there were only three acceptable answers when the commander called you on the carpet: "yes, sir," "no, sir" and "no excuse, sir."

Nowhere is "no excuse, sir" more appropriate than in response to the disgraceful treatment we now know that many of our wounded soldiers have been getting.

"No excuse, sir," across the board: from an administration that forgot "support the troops" is more than a bumper sticker; to a military that tried to blame it all on low-ranking sergeants.

To a Veterans Administration whose leaders tried to play down the number of serious injuries, yet were so unfamiliar with their own system that, too many times, the injured were sent to facilities unequipped to treat their particular injuries.

And, yes, to a Congress and news media that should have uncovered this long ago.

Only three people rise above this mess: *Washington Post* reporters Dana Priest and Anne Hull, and the remarkable Bob Woodruff of ABC News.

The Posties did what the rest of us didn't. When they heard the rumors, they took the time to check them out. Not rocket science, just the first obligation of journalism.

Then there is Woodruff, who went to Iraq to get one story, was badly wounded and after months of treatment recovered to find another: the unacceptable way that many who suffered the kind of serious brain injury he suffered were lost in a nightmare of red tape and going without the treatment they needed.

The rest of us should have paid more attention. We can only be grateful to three who did.

—March 4, 2006

Sharing the Sacrifice

Retired Air Force Lieutenant General Charles Roadman is part of a distinguished panel of experts investigating the problems at Walter Reed Hospital, and what he said the other day caught my eye.

One problem, he told the *Washington Post*, is that Iraq is producing so *many* casualties. "The nation," he said, "needs to realize we are at war."

As I read that, I wondered, how many of us lead lives completely untouched by this war?

It is being fought by an all-volunteer force that accounts for less than one-half of one percent of us. Nor do many of us feel the economic impact since it is being fought mostly on borrowed money.

If we closed our eyes to TV and newspapers, most of us could get through the day without knowing there *was* a war.

When I was a child, we all knew about World War II. It was fought by draftees, and everyone had a dad or an uncle or cousin or neighbor who was gone to war. Food was rationed, taxes were high. Every day brought something to remind us we were at war.

These days some Americans may not even *know* anyone in the military, let alone have a connection.

Our volunteer military is the best in the world, but again I wonder, should democracies fight wars with an all-volunteer force?

Should we *ever* go to war unless *all* of us are willing to share the sacrifice?

—April 5, 2007

More Than Lip Service

I had breakfast the other day with the ambassador from one of America's strongest and closest allies. We got to talking about Iraq and Vietnam, and he asked me what I thought the great lessons of those years have been.

I said, first, that we can help people, but we can't do it for them, and, second, that America leads best when it leads by example— when we demonstrate how our system works by practicing what we preach, not by resorting to the methods of those who oppose us.

"May I suggest one more thing?" he asked. "That America is most successful when it does not work alone, but with its friends.

"America has the strongest economy in the world and without question the most powerful military, but when it has tried to work alone, it has seldom been able to work its will," he continued. "Yet when it has been able to forge broad coalitions, it has seldom failed."

That is more than opinion. It's just a fact, which makes me wonder, even at this eleventh hour, shouldn't that be the focus of our Iraq policy? Bringing together a broad coalition of Western nations and Iraq's neighbors to contain the war and pressure its warring factions to settle their differences?

Instead, we have paid lip service to diplomacy, made the debate about battlefield tactics and searched for a military solution to a political problem.

So far, we haven't found one.

—*May 27, 2007*

Is Baghdad Too Hot for Iraqi Leaders?

I am still not sure that I believe it: the Iraqi parliament is going on vacation during the month of August.

The White House offers the lame excuse that, after all, Baghdad is hot in August—sometimes 130 degrees.

May I ask a follow-up?

How much hotter do you suppose it is if you are wearing a helmet and full-body armor, carrying ammunition and walking foot patrols through Baghdad?

The last I heard, that is how American troops are spending their August in Iraq.

For me, this does it.

God help the Iraqi people, because there is not much America can do to help a government that leaves Americans dying in the streets while the parliament escapes to cooler climes.

Does this mean we should pull out immediately?

No. A sudden withdrawal could set the entire region aflame. The truth is there are no good options left. But from here on, we need to put aside the dream of building a democracy in Iraq and focus solely on what is in our national interest.

It won't be pretty, but for all our good intentions, about all we can do now is try to contain this mess, pull our troops back from the middle of this civil war and concentrate instead on the terrorist threat that this country faces around the world.

As for what kind of government Iraq needs, let their parliament figure it out. They can get right on it when the Baghdad weather turns cooler.

—*July 15, 2007*

Asking the Right Questions About Iraq

For months now, the administration has been telling us, let's wait until we hear from General Petraeus before we decide where to go next in Iraq.

Well, tomorrow we hear.

The atmosphere is much like the time during the Vietnam War, when the commander then, General William Westmoreland, was brought home to answer the question: Are we winning?

He assured us we were, and the government offered a blizzard of statistics to back him up. They weren't wrong. They were just irrelevant.

All we really learned then is that we were asking the wrong question. When we have to ask, "Are we winning?" we're probably losing. Victory is always obvious.

The right question would have been: Is it worth the cost?

America eventually concluded it was not, and we left the war.

Let me preempt that question to General Petraeus. We haven't lost this war, but we're not winning it. We're hanging on. Victory would be obvious. Iraqi families would be strolling the streets of Baghdad, and Osama bin Laden would be walking out of a cave somewhere with his hands up.

Instead of that question, let's hope the general will be asked what we so often forgot during Vietnam: Is this worth the cost in lives and money?

And here's a follow-up: when the Iraqi parliament went on vacation during August, I gave up on trying to help them find a way to have an effective government. They have to do that. What we need to know now is whether keeping a large American military force in Iraq is the best way to make America safer.

To me, that's the real question.

—September 9, 2007

A Tragedy Waiting
to Happen

———

The worst thing about that report that fourteen Iraqi civilians had been killed in Baghdad by members of a private American security firm called Blackwater is that this was a tragedy waiting to happen.

Because, as we now know, private security firms like Blackwater have been operating above the law, setting their own rules outside the military chain of command, and the government knew it. Their job was to protect key civilians, and as long as they got it done, no one asked questions.

How can that be?

It's another of those shortcuts we've become so accustomed to in this war—dangerous times require extraordinary methods. It's also a lot cheaper, which is why we have contracted out more than a hundred thousand jobs normally done by soldiers to private contractors in Iraq. It's easier all round; the military has all those rules and regulations and benefits.

It also makes it look like our force in Iraq is a lot smaller than it really is.

It's a bargain, all right, until something like the recent tragedy, which sets the whole effort back.

May I have a drumroll here for the clichés—because apparently they were forgotten along the way:

- Lord Acton said, "Power corrupts, absolute power corrupts absolutely."

- And then there was your high school civics teacher, who told us how the founders came up with the idea of checks and balances on power.
- And here's one more: you get what you pay for.

Everything needs a check. When there are no checks, things get out of balance. And will we ever learn there are no bargains in war? You have to do it right, to get it right.

—October 7, 2007

Do We No Longer
Practice What
We Preach?

E dward R. Murrow was one of the first to understand the power of worldwide communications.

But it was the message, not the power to reach so many, that concerned him.

His biographer Alexander Kendrick said that, like Thoreau nearly a century before him, Murrow asked himself "whether Maine had anything to say to Texas," and when he became head of the U.S. Information Agency, whether the United States had anything to say to the rest of the world.

Murrow concluded the answer was "Yes."

I thought about that as we learned more about the CIA's use of what our own army and the Geneva Conventions define as torture, and how officials destroyed evidence when a federal judge demanded tapes of the interrogation episodes.

Is *that* our message to the world? That we are a government of laws except when it is "inconvenient"?

If so, then what was done in the name of security has greatly *harmed* security.

Weapons keep our enemies at bay, but our real security rests on whether the rest of the world comes to share our values, or the values of those who oppose us and whether all people are better served by a government of laws or what someone decides the law ought to be at some particular moment.

Have we helped our cause with the rest of the world when they come to believe we have sunk to using the tactics of those who hate us, when we no longer can be trusted to practice what we preach?

Is this what we want the world to know?

More importantly, is it what we want our children to know?

—December 9, 2007

VII

SEASONS

I was talking to a group of journalism students one day, and during the question period one of them said, "You talked a lot about how much fun it is to be a reporter. Is there a downside? What's bad about it?"

It didn't take me long to answer that.

"Sometimes, you get to work on Christmas," I said. "News never goes on vacation, or follows a schedule."

Maybe the reason I have always loved the holidays is because I had to work on so many of them during my early days. Before I was married, I worked a lot of Christmases, "because you don't have a family." Well, I guess not, if you don't count a mom and a brother and sister. One year after I was married with two kids, I was stuck in Plains, Georgia, covering Jimmy Carter, and my wife, Pat, and two young daughters flew in so we could have Thanksgiving dinner together. We wound up at the local McDonald's, which was the only restaurant we could find open. We hadn't quite finished the fries when my older daughter said, "Can we go back home now?" You don't forget such moments.

More than once over the years, we rearranged the family Christmas festivities to accommodate Dad's work schedule. I spent one New Year's Eve in Iran while Pat went to bed with a good book back in Washington.

We've stopped counting missed birthdays and anniversaries. Pat threw a huge bash for my last one, but I was in New Hampshire and missed hers this year. (Actually, I missed my own birthday party one year when I got stuck in New York, and Pat served birthday cake to my all-male poker group. They had a great time, I was told.)

Whatever the reasons, the holiday lights at Christmas, the thought of a big meal at Thanksgiving or just seeing the grandkids' faces as any holiday approaches puts me in a better mood, and I have written about holidays many times over the years.

Sometimes, the holiday spirit has even brought out the poet in me.

Poetry on Face the Nation?

Absolutely!

To paraphrase Mel Brooks, it is good to be the anchorman.

The Christmas Story

If I wished you a merry Christmas, some would say, "Well, how improper. He's throwing his religion in my face."

But I hope I'm not, because to me the Christmas story is a message of love and forgiveness. To me, that means tolerance and respect for others. These are wonderful thoughts, but no more admirable than Judaism's emphasis on values or Islam's command to help the poor, which to me are just different ways of saying the same thing.

I have come to believe that all the great religions are basically true, all part of the same piece, a conclusion I neither ask nor expect anyone to share. If it matters to you, I am a believer but, like Kierkegaard, I am suspicious of all organized religion because too often it professes to know the mind of God and who could know that? To me, the greatest misunderstanding of religion is held by those who try to impose their beliefs on others and teach their children they are somehow superior to those who do not believe as they believe, which would seem to miss the point of all religion.

Rather than arguing over the details, wouldn't we all be better off to focus on the values that all great religions share? We'll find out later who got the details right. The one sure thing I know about all this is that the Christmas story helps me. It reminds me that I am happier when I try to be forgiving rather than revengeful, when I try to be helpful instead of judgmental.

So I do wish you a merry Christmas, if you know what I mean.

—December 19, 2004

Not-So-Happy Holidays

M y grandchildren came home from kindergarten with a question: Why couldn't we celebrate Hanukkah and Christmas like their friend Isabel?

Good question. Wouldn't all of us, believers and nonbelievers, agree that a certain truth runs through all three of the great religions, Judaism, Christianity and Islam—that love is more powerful than hate, and that we are better off if we treat others as we wish to be treated?

So why shouldn't we learn from and celebrate something from all religions? And why do we so often forget that part and become bogged down in arguments over details?

Like last week, when our White House correspondent Bill Plante reported the president, a proud Evangelical Christian, is getting grief from those who believe his Christmas card is not Christmasy enough because it just says "Happy Holidays."

Bill pointed out the card does contain scripture from the Hebrew Bible, what Christians call the Old Testament, which, he noted, gives the card a sort of diversity insurance.

As I often do when politicians claim to know God's views, I called my source upstairs to double-check. Not to brag, but my sources up there are usually as good as those of the politicians and TV preachers. And, sure enough, when I asked what the feeling in heaven was about Christmas cards, my heavenly source just laughed.

"Frankly," he said, "we're more into the big picture up here. But the important thing to know about this is that God does have a divine sense of humor.

"After all," he said, "why else would he put up with you?"

He had me there.

—*December 11, 2005*

Twice on Valentine's Day, I have resorted to little rhymes
to wish our viewers a happy day. On February 13, 2005,
I reminded them that the most powerful sentence in
the English language has only three words—I love you—
and I reminded them as well that like most
powerful things, it is often difficult to see and
even harder to know.

Valentine's Day

A child's question asked of me,
If I can't see it, can it be?
I see my toy, I know it's there.
I feel my arm, I touch my hair.
These are things I know to be
But are there things I cannot see?
What of the wind, where does it go?
Are there other things to know?
Oh yes, my dear, and soon you'll find

They're locked inside the heart and mind.
Sweet love's desire, a mother's prayer
More real than all we see out there.
More real than sun and moon and rain,
At first much harder to explain.
The only thing that I can say
I say it now in just this way:
What is real and what is not?
Love is real, the rest is not.

Two years later, on February 11, 2007, I penned this
ode to a most unhappy fellow.

The Man Who
Forgot Valentine

Valentine's Day is next Wednesday, I hear.
So write it down 'cause I know this is true.
To forget Valentine is a felony crime
To every woman that I ever knew.
A good woman's love is the best thing there is,
But an old guy like me understands,
Forget Valentine and she'll turn on a dime.
You'll have a loon astronaut on your hands.
Late getting home, lamp shade for a hat,

They'll let it go once, maybe twice.
But no Valentine, hon? I suggest that you run.
That butcher knife is ready to slice.
On a hill far away where the grass is so green,
Is the grave of a well-meaning guy.
Carved there on his stone that stands all alone
As a warning for all who pass by:
"Had I written it down, I wouldn't be here.
They wouldn't have needed this shrine.
Because I am the one, poor son of a gun:
The man who forgot Valentine."

Friends Like These

For Christians and Jews, these are holy days, and as each day of the week passed, I was reminded just how diverse a country we have become.

A friend begged off dinner at midweek after realizing she had to work late because she was the only person in the office not celebrating Passover. Payback, really. Her colleagues had worked Christmas, but I know she wouldn't think of it that way. Just a nice thing to do for friends.

A Muslim friend called my wife to wish us a happy Easter. A small gesture, but appreciated. After all, he was calling about our holiday, not his, but it made me remember—as the Muslims would say—that we are all people of the Book whose religious traditions evolve from the same God.

A friend who has a mixed marriage told me about spending the middle of the week teaching her kids to make matzo balls and most of yesterday dyeing Easter eggs.

One day the children will sort out the details. For now they are learning the traditions of two great religions. Another friend who is not so sure of God still hides eggs for her kids who are teenagers. Not such a bad thing, either.

Down through the ages, people have argued over the differences and details of religion. How much better it is when we respect the beliefs of others, remember the common values that all religions share and try to emulate those values in our daily lives.

In ways large and small, my friends reminded me of that this week. I'm glad I have friends like that.

—April 16, 2006

Mother's Day

Milton Berle used to tell the story of how his mother saw all his performances, led the laughter, stared down those who didn't laugh and once, when a drunk in the audience made a pass at her, did nothing until he finished his act. She wasn't about to draw attention from her son. But once he left the stage, she pummeled the man with her fists and bit him. Only a mother.

And don't all of us remember a similar story about our own mothers, who always find a way to give us the credit and to be proud of us, no matter what we do? Most of us remember the love, but we sometimes forget the work that mothers do.

Being a mom requires, first of all, time—not the so-called quality time, but unending time that comes from putting the kids first.

I know a mom with two preteen sons whose recent Saturday

schedule included five separate games—three soccer matches, two baseball games. I know a mother of two teenagers who says, "I love baseball, but there are so many games, I sometimes pray for rain." I know a new mother of twins who says, "This would be easy if I could just get one night of uninterrupted sleep." But she knows that is years away. And none of them would trade their lives for any other. What mothers know of love others can only surmise.

So on Mother's Day, we take a break from the news to say thanks and to wish them happiness, a good night's rest and the joy that comes from the occasional summer rain.

Five years later, I turned once more to rhyme.

WHAT IS THERE TO SAY ABOUT MOMS?

What is there to say about Moms that hasn't been said before?
Here's just a couple of things, maybe three or four.
When you were just a little one,
Who was it that taught you a song?
And even more important,
The difference 'tween right and wrong?
When others turned against you,
Who was always there?
Who always took your side
No matter when or where?

If you're like me it was Mom.

Who kept the family going
Whether times were good or not?
Who always could remember

The things that we forgot
Birthdays, homework deadlines
A hundred things or more.
And on school days, wide awake or not
Got you out the door?

If you're like me it was Mom.

Who told you you were just as good
As any rich man's son?
And not to look for some excuse
To do what needed done.
You've known movers and shakers
Some may even know you.
But in the final accounting,
Who taught you most that's true?

If you're like me it was Mom.
                              —May 13, 2001, and May 14, 2006

Graduation Day

—————

Yesterday I gave the commencement address at the Lyndon B. Johnson School of Public Affairs at the University of Texas in Austin.

I told the students it was a special honor for me because Lyndon Johnson was the first politician I ever saw—I was ten years old, he was campaigning for the Senate and came to our neighborhood in a helicopter.

We had never seen a helicopter, and when we heard his voice on an electric bullhorn come out of the sky, it scared us to death. We didn't know if it was Lyndon Johnson, or God, or what—but that's another story.

What made yesterday even more meaningful for me was that my parents grew up on the edge of that campus during the Great Depression.

It might well have been a thousand miles away because they had no money to go there, but seeing that their children would have what they couldn't—a college education—became the driving force in their lives.

I was the first on either side of the family to achieve that, and a week ago, when my nephew received his degree, their dream was realized and then some. Not only had all their children graduated from college, but their grandchildren had as well.

It made me so proud because I know how they would have felt. That's the thing about graduations—whether you're a graduate or a parent or a sister or brother or someone who just dropped by, graduations bring out feelings we experience at no other time of our lives.

—*May 30, 2007*

*The war in Iraq had dragged on far longer than anyone
had anticipated when I wrote this in 2005.*

Code of Honor

The other night I went to a screening of *Faith of Our Fathers*, the
new movie about John McCain's five-year ordeal in a North
Vietnamese prison. It airs on A&E tomorrow night.

It flashes back to McCain's high school days when the principal
reported bad grades to his dad, whose only question was not about
grades but whether his son had violated the school honor code—had
he lied or cheated?

When told he had not, his father said, "Well, call me if he does."

McCain says that code of honor drilled into him by his father
and the Naval Academy is why he was able to survive the torture
and inhumanity of his prison captors. He couldn't let his father
down. That code of honor was the center of his life that gave him
strength—what separated him from his captors.

I thought about that as yet another tale of torture and abuse came
out about the POW camp *we* are running at Guantánamo Bay.

Columnist Tom Friedman said the prison ought to be shut down
because the stories about it are so inflaming the Arab world, they're
making the war on terrorism more dangerous for American soldiers.

But as I watched the McCain movie, I wondered if the greater
danger is the impact Guantánamo is having on us—Do we want our
children to believe this is how we are? Is this the honor code we are
passing on to the next generation?

As we reflect on the meaning of Memorial Day, let us remember first what it is that separates us from those who would take our freedom—what John McCain's dad taught his kid, what we should be teaching ours.

—*May 9, 2005*

"Dad, Please Just Act Normal"

———

You can look it up: more telephone calls are made on Mother's Day than any other day of the year. It's a sweet thing to know. Moms deserve it. But what day would you guess that most of the collect calls are made? You got it. Father's Day. Paying the bills is just one part of being a dad.

Fatherhood, as every dad knows, is an evolving process. In the early years, we're adored, the ultimate authority on everything. But as our children grow older, that changes. By the teenage years, they begin to suspect we don't know anything. It's as if we somehow became adults without experiencing anything having to do with school, sports, driving, music or certainly the opposite sex.

I'll never forget the first boy-girl party at our house. Mom was complimented on how nice she looked. My instructions were, "Dad, please just act normal." And has a father, any father, ever told a joke that caused a teenager to laugh? "Dad, at least try to act normal."

So for all the dads, a toast on our day, and some good news if you're still in that stage where you're an embarrassment to the entire family: that, too, passes. Before long, the kids will be telling you again how smart you are, even if they don't believe it, but because they really love you. Or maybe because they've discovered they have learned a little something from you. That's going to make you proud, but by then, you'll know you've learned a lot from them, too.

So, Dads, enjoy the day, but, remember, act normal and don't forget to pick up the check.

—June 17, 2001

The Name of the Day

There is plenty of bad news, but in thousands of homes across America last week, it could not match the good news, because in those homes a tiny face looked into a big face, smiled and said, "Da-da."

Ask anyone who heard those words if anything more important than that happened. If you heard it for the first time, you were officially eligible to celebrate Father's Day. But there's more. Those words begin the process of renaming everyone in the family. Grown-ups who thought they did the naming soon come to understand it's the little people who co-opt the naming rights.

My wife didn't want to name our daughters after her, because she didn't want to be known as Big Pat.

So we named our youngest after my sister, who soon became Big Sharon, which Little Sharon shortened to Biggie, which stuck. That could change, however. At age four, Little Sharon said that when she had a daughter, she would name her Little Sharon, so she could be Big Sharon, which would make Biggie, Old Sharon. The hazards of the name game.

We name our pets, but it is said that pets give each other names that only they know, which makes me wonder. Whatever our worldly fame, are the names given us by the innocent the names by which God knows us? We won't know that for a while. So to all the grand-pas and granddads and big daddies and big papas and papaws and poopsies and pops, popos and bobos and all the dads and daddies, don't let the bad news take your mind off the good news.

Have a great—well, have a great Bobo Day.

—June 15, 2003

Present at the Beginning

F ireworks are great, but here is a better way to celebrate the Fourth of July: read about it, because there are some great new reasons to do that—two terrific books, *Founding Brothers* by Joseph Ellis, which came out last year, and David McCullough's spectacular new biography of John Adams.

Thomas Paine, the great voice of liberty, thought the founding of America was inevitable. After all, he reasoned, "No island could long rule a continent." But as Ellis and McCullough remind us in these books, accomplishing the inevitable in this case was no small task.

Even as we celebrate the courage and wisdom of the founders, we sometimes forget just what a long shot America was. There have been many revolutions since ours, but think of this: before ours, no people had ever broken away from a colonial power.

Those present at the beginning of our revolution had no idea how it would come out. But they risked their lives and fortunes because they believed they were right and thought that if they could explain the reasons for the revolution, they would succeed.

Even before they raised an army, in one document Thomas Jefferson codified as no one ever had the common yearning of all people to be free. That yearning drove the revolution, and when the world understood that, America's cause was every person's cause. The world changed forever.

Today America stands as history's oldest and most enduring republic. These are books about the remarkable people who did all that. As McCullough writes, "I don't think we can ever know enough about them." Nor do I.

—*July 1, 2007*

On another Fourth.

Checks and Balances

O n this day we remember that tiny group who pledged their lives, their fortunes and their sacred honor to do what no one else of their day thought possible: defeat the greatest military power in the world and form their own nation.

Reading Ron Chernow's excellent new biography of Alexander Hamilton has reminded me of one part of their story that is often forgotten: just how much some of them disliked each other and how suspicious all of them were of human nature.

They were determined that no one of them and no part of their new government would ever corner all the power. They had united to throw out the British, but they almost went to war among themselves over how to divide that power. The way Madison saw it, you wouldn't need a government if men were angels, and if the governors were angels, you wouldn't need controls or restraints on them. But they were dealing with men, not angels, and so they devised the ingenious system of checks and balances.

As I was thinking about their remarkable insight into human behavior, I wondered who among us they would have admired.

Here's my guess: Supreme Court Justice Sandra Day O'Connor, for one. When the court ruled last week that even prisoners at Guantánamo Bay have a right to their day in court, she wrote, "A state of war is not a blank check for the president when it comes to the rights of the nation's citizens." The founders would have recognized that she was speaking their language—a good thing for us to recognize, as well, on this fine day.

—July 4, 2004

Saying Thanks for Thanksgiving

Of all the holidays, Thanksgiving is my favorite. The pilgrims held the first one, two hundred years later Abraham Lincoln made it official, and we've marked the occasion ever since with a nice, large second helping.

Christmas has its music. The Fourth has fireworks, but we celebrate Thanksgiving by doing what we shouldn't—eating too much.

Maybe that's why it is so much fun. Thanksgiving is the one holiday that is not about someone or something else. It's just about us, our families, and if they include grandchildren, God's preview of heaven, it's all the better.

So we gather with no purpose but to be together, say thanks and dive into a great meal.

Like an aircraft carrier that leaves port only when surrounded by smaller ships, Thanksgiving arrives surrounded by a flotilla of smaller holidays that are observed with the same discipline and ritual. Wednesday has become getaway day, the busiest travel day of the year; Friday is leftover day for the stay-at-homes, and Black Friday for the shoppers.

And then there is today, Sunday, when millions sigh and say of their recent visitors, "We love 'em, but thank heaven they're finally out of here. Now we can relax and get back to normal."

How to celebrate that? Go to the fridge right now and see if there is enough left to scrape together a little turkey soup. It's great on a cold night.

—November 27, 2005

And Speaking of Food . . .

I want to tell you first that if you did not get a flu shot, go get one. I put mine off this year and got blindsided by the strain of flu that's going around, and trust me, you want no part of this stuff. But even in the worst storm, there's always a little ray of sunshine, and one day, when I was trying to think of something, anything, that might taste good to eat, my wife suggested an old-fashioned grilled-cheese sandwich.

Well, in our low-cal, watch-your-weight world, I can't remember when I last ate a grilled-cheese sandwich. It was like being reintroduced to an old friend that you'd lost contact with for no good reason. And I'll tell you, they're still as good as ever—better, maybe. Grilled and a little butter, and when it's on whole-grain bread, the grains get crunchy, where the cheese gets gooey and warm.

So here's my message for the holidays: get yourself that flu shot and celebrate with a grilled-cheese sandwich, then you'll be big and strong and ready for the millennium.

—December 19, 1999

VIII

WHO WE ARE

W as it Yogi Berra who said, "You can see a lot by looking"? If he didn't, he should have. I've spent a lot of my life as a reporter just looking and listening.

I suppose reporters are professional observers, if there is such a thing, but I was an observer long before I was a reporter. I must have picked up the habit from my mother, who loved to people-watch and had an incredible sense of recall. She could walk through a room and remember where every piece of furniture was placed, every picture on the wall and what every person in the room was wearing.

It may also have had something to do with my Texas roots. My friend Dan Jenkins, the novelist who, like me, comes from Fort Worth, once said that for some inexplicable reason looking out the window was a "major league pastime" there. I never saw the data he based that on, but I've enjoyed looking out a lot of windows in my time.

My recall was never as good as my mother's, but I have come to understand the power (and the pleasure) of observation, and the thing I have never tired of observing is the American people.

I love travel and I have reported over the years from many places around the world. Yet it was always America and its ways that fascinated me most. I spent most of my life as a beat reporter: the police station and the courthouse in the old days, later the Pentagon, the White House, the State Department and Capitol Hill, but my real beat was America, and most of what I learned about the American people, I learned by the simple act of watching—watching what we held dear and memorialized, the sports we played and how we played them, what we read, who we *chose as heroes, how we treated the least among us, how we grew up and raised our children and how we dealt with growing old.*

Monday through Friday, I wrote thousands of stories mainly about the process of government for CBS News, but as I looked back at the hundreds of essays I wrote for Face the Nation, *I discovered that the themes I most often returned to on Sundays were the ones I loved the most—the American people and how we came to be who we are.*

Paula Jones was one of the women who accused
Bill Clinton of improper advances when he was
governor. When her story became known in 1997,
it set off a blizzard of accusations that led to the Monica
Lewinsky scandal. I found liitle to admire in Paula
Jones, but I was appalled at how we allowed the story
to wrongly stereotype thousands of Americans who
happened to be poor.

Trailer Trash

I 'm going to say a word about, of all things, people who live in trailer parks. As mainstream publications published their advance stories this week about the Paula Jones case, I noticed any number of references to "trailer park trash," "white trailer trash" and quotes about "You never know what you'll find when you drag a hundred-dollar bill through a trailer park."

Put aside that Paula Jones didn't live in a trailer, but at a time when we've carried political correctness to nausea-inducing levels, it is a little surprising that we find nothing wrong with stereotyping people by neighborhood. Maybe it shouldn't be surprising, because it's just another way to make fun of the poor, the only group in public relations–conscious America anymore that has no spokesman or advocate to fight back.

The Reverend Nathan Baxter, the dean of Washington's National Cathedral, noted recently that after the civil rights movement, every sociopolitical movement in America has been by and for the middle- and upper-middle-class professional community. They're good causes all, but in each of them, you don't see many poor people involved.

It should be noted that living in a trailer park doesn't happen because people are genetically character-flawed; it is because they can't afford to live anyplace else. I would also add that I know a lot of nice people who lived in trailer parks, and I know some real trash that lived in big houses.

—*January 12, 1997*

Sophistries

While I was on vacation, I read a fine little mystery novel called *Sophie's World* by a Norwegian writer named Jostein Gaarder. It is about a mysterious stranger who teaches a young girl named Sophie about the history of philosophy, and at one point he explains how the first real philosopher, Socrates, lived in a time when the population of Athens included a large professional class known as Sophists, men who were debaters, men who earned handsome fees by helping others win arguments.

Since the money was in winning the argument, not in finding the truth, Sophie learns the Sophists soon became self-opinionated know-it-alls who went around looking for arguments, so satisfied with their own limited knowledge that they were not the least bit embarrassed to claim they knew everything about many things they hadn't the faintest notion of.

Does any of that sound familiar these days, when filing lawsuits has become the national hobby and it sometimes seems that one American in three has his or her own talk show and where everyone who speaks has all the answers all the time?

Sophie learns that what set Socrates apart was that he understood that he knew very little. But it troubled him so much he tried to learn more.

Wouldn't it be refreshing to hear those who have access to public forums these days admit they don't have all the answers but are working hard to find them?

Wouldn't all of us be better off if we did that, even journalists?

—*July 9, 1995*

Talk to Your Kids

An organization called The Partnership for a Drug-Free America ran a full-page ad in newspapers yesterday titled "How to Talk to Your Kids About Drugs." It was such good advice on how to broach a difficult subject with anyone that I want to share part of it with you.

First, the ad advises parents not to worry about where to start—start anywhere; pertinent advice when we think of all the times we've put off a difficult subject by telling ourselves, "I just don't know where to begin." It reminds me of a long-ago news conference at the Nixon White House when Henry Kissinger tried to dodge a tough question by saying it was hard to begin to answer because time didn't allow for a complete explanation, to which reporter Helen Thomas said, "Then start at the end."

The ad also reminds us that talking to someone doesn't mean doing all the talking.

It is much more important to listen, which is the only part of a conversation where we learn anything. When you've been a reporter as long as I have, you understand that more than most.

I've gotten a scoop or two along the way, but when I think of the stories I've missed, it was usually because I wasn't listening when someone was trying to tell me something.

The most important thing the ad says is to remember that if you don't talk to your kids, others with strong opinions will: those who use drugs and those who sell them. And I would just add, if you don't believe that, ask your kids.

—January 5, 1997

O.J. and D.C.

S tate of the Union Speech Night gives Washington a chance to strut its stuff, and Washington just loves it.

Presidents never look more presidential than when they're standing before that flag speaking to Washington's A-list. It's Congress's favorite night because it allows members to get on TV back home with their reactions to the president's proposals.

So when the O.J. trial verdict interrupted Washington's big night out, Washington took it hard. Lawmakers were convinced they'd be crowded right off the news, and many were. Keeping a stiff upper lip, one actually told our reporter, "In politics, as in life, you can't control events. You just have to keep moving forward."

Hey, Congressman, we're not talking death in the family here, just a heavy news day.

In any case, we should thank Frank Rich of the *New York Times* for noticing what the rest of us missed in all the bedlam: it wasn't a collision of two stories that night, but two parts of the same story. For all our progress on race relations, a report on the State of the

Union that glosses over the divide that still exists between black and white Americans is incomplete at best.

The president and J. C. Watts, the African-American congress-man who gave the Republican response, tiptoed around the subject. But then along came O.J., again, reminding us just how differently black and white Americans see many things these days.

Consider these poll findings. When jurors at his criminal trial found Simpson not guilty, three-fourths of white Americans thought the jury got it wrong. After the latest trial, three-fourths of black Americans thought the jury erred.

Here's a prediction: in a few years, few will remember what the president or J. C. Watts said, but in a hundred years, historians will cite the O. J. Simpson trial as an example of the divide between black and white Americans at the close of the twentieth century. If that's wrong, call me in a hundred years and I'll correct it.

—*February 9, 1997*

It's not a hundred years yet, but I think I am
already right, at least on the part about
Clinton and J. C. Watts.

The Congress finally banned tobacco ads on TV but the
pro-smoking gang went down swinging, claiming
at one point that advertising didn't really encourage
kids to smoke.

The Hit Parade

For those of my generation, tobacco advertising was a part of our lives for so long we hardly knew it was there, like traffic noise when you've lived in the city long enough.

One of my earliest memories of childhood is being at my grand-mother's in the days before television when our family would gather around the radio. We loved the Lucky Strike Hit Parade, and I can still remember the Lucky slogan, LSMFT, Lucky Strike Means Fine Tobacco. And when World War II came and Lucky switched from a green to a white pack, I can remember the radio telling us, "Lucky Strike green has gone to war," whatever that meant.

Does advertising encourage kids to smoke? I've run no surveys, but that was all a long time ago, and I can still remember it, so it must have had some impact on me.

By the time I got to college and was on the way to a three-pack-a-day habit, I was being told that "Winstons Taste Good, Like a Ciga-rette Should."

And being a kid in Fort Worth, I was extra proud that the Marlboro Man was really a cowboy who worked on a ranch just north of town.

It was all around us, wherever we looked or listened, those images of the smart people, the people we wanted to be like, doing what seemed so natural, smoking.

I finally quit in 1974, the year that Joe Camel was born. What helped the most was when someone gave me another image to think about: "How can smoking be a natural thing to do?" he said. "Did you ever see an animal try to pick up something on fire and put it in its mouth?"

I don't know yet if the tobacco deal announced this week is the right deal, but if a way has been found to get rid of tobacco advertising, it will be fine with me. What a con.

—June 22, 1997

News item: Fort Worth, Texas: A gunman walked into a church Wednesday night, opened fire with an automatic weapon and killed seven people. He gave no explanation before killing himself.

Common Sense

If you had a two-year-old, what would you do about such things as prescription drugs, drain cleaner, kitchen knives and other household necessities that pose a danger to children? You wouldn't stop buying them. You'd just put them out of reach on a higher shelf.

And what would you do when that child got old enough to drive? Say no and sell the family car?

No, most parents would teach the child to drive and would not think twice about the law requiring a driver's license. Just common sense, which makes me wonder why we refuse to take the same commonsense approach when it comes to dealing with guns.

Fort Worth is where I grew up, so for me the tragedy hit home, literally, and afterward I found myself asking the same question, why?

What could possibly cause a person to do such a thing? It's the wrong question, of course. The actions of the deranged, by definition, do not make sense.

The harder question is: Why was it so easy for a deranged man to arm himself with lethal weapons? Had he walked in with a tire tool or even an axe, most of those people would not be dead.

It is not a question of taking guns from sportsmen or legitimate gun owners, as the professional gun lobbyists would have you believe.

But in a nation of 270 million people, there is a small percentage, which is a sizable group, who are mentally disturbed. That's only natural.

In light of that, should we not be as careful about who owns a gun as we are about who owns and drives a car?

We wouldn't question for a moment putting rat poison beyond the reach of a two-year-old.

Why is it so hard for us to put guns on a higher shelf?

—September 19, 1999

In the closing days of 2007, Congress reached a
compromise with the NRA and passed legislation that
had been lying dormant for five years that made it more
difficult for the mentally deranged to buy firearms.

The Baseball Lesson

I f you want to spot-check on just how tangled up we're becoming over what's important, I refer you to a story in the *New York Times* last week that tells how more and more parents are paying professional instructors $70 an hour to teach ten-year-old Little Leaguers how to hit a baseball.

School counselors told the *Times* it is just another sign of how competitive childhood has become and how parents feel compelled to give their children every edge in both academics and athletics.

The parents say it's about self-esteem; striking out is just too hard on kids, they say, and besides, it reduces the inevitable fights when a parent tries to teach a child something.

Maybe so, but I think they're missing one of the best parts of being a parent and the whole point of what baseball is about.

Baseball is about learning to deal with failure.

In baseball, even the best fail more than they succeed.

Baseball's strength has always been that one generation passed it on to another, passed on its traditions and its secrets.

Fathers taught sons, and now daughters, and along the way, they found something they can talk about, even in those years when they have nothing else to share.

Long ago, when I was a sore-arm catcher on the freshman team at Texas Christian University, I threw out two runners who tried to steal on me. And after the game, my dad said, "Bobby, you might be a ballplayer yet."

Not long after that, my arm finally gave out, my baseball dreams ended forever, and the next year, my dad died. But every time I think of him, the first thing I always remember is what he said that day on the ball field and how good it made me feel.

—June 27, 1999

The twentieth was about to become the twenty-first...

A Century's Work

When I was a boy, the turn of the century seemed a long way off; so far away, I couldn't really imagine it. I can remember writing down 2000, which just didn't look right, and then subtracting 1937, the year I was born. And then looking at the answer and saying, "That's so far off and I'll be so old, I probably won't even know about it."

Well, it turns out the arithmetic was right, but lo and behold, I am able to get around unassisted, testament to the most important thing this century brought, the remarkable advances in living conditions that led to longer life spans.

We're living thirty years longer on average than the people at the beginning of this century.

We're living better, too, and not just materially. We have changed the relationship between blacks and whites and men and women, and that was for the better.

Our parents beat the Nazis and we won the Cold War, and that's not bad for a century's work. And it probably was the American century; certainly ours as much as anyone else's.

The one thing that does worry me is we seem to be much ruder to each other than we used to be. Whether it's road rage or the new determination to never give an inch or our current insistence on always having the last word, we have too many times become too ill-mannered and impatient for our own well-being. We ought to work on that. But in the meantime, I'm just proud to be here.

—*December 26, 1999*

Now this is good news!

The Nation Faces Us

I wake up early, and for as long as I can remember, the first thing that comes to my mind is, I wonder what's in the paper this morning. My routine never varies. I scan the headlines while I make the coffee, and for the next hour or so, my wife and I read the paper. It's our favorite part of the day.

The golf teacher Harvey Penick once said, "Anyone who likes golf is my friend." And I'm that way about anyone who likes the news. Frankly, those who don't, mystify me, which brings me to this: last week, seventeen students from the Advanced Placement government class at a Kutztown, Pennsylvania, high school got up at 3 A.M. and drove to Washington to tell me their weekly assignment for the last two years has been to watch *Face the Nation*, and then discuss it in class.

Now that may sound like cruel and unusual punishment, but I

wish you could have met these kids. They asked the kind of questions I usually get from college graduate students. They knew more about the government than some reporters I know. I give *Face the Nation* about one percent of the credit for this. The rest goes to their teacher, Barry Adams, who, it quickly became obvious to me, has that gift of all great teachers, the enthusiasm and the ability to make learning fun.

On the way out, one of the kids asked me if I thought adults knew there really are young people out there who care about their government. Well, if I didn't know it before, I know it now, and that's the best news I've heard in a long time.

—*April 1, 2001*

It became a school tradition, and they've
come every year since.

Good Schools

W atching the Senate haggle this week over how much money to set aside to improve our schools caused me to wonder: Why are we so reluctant to spend money on education? We all agree it's important. We all say our kids come first. Yet our schools are always strapped for cash. There are probably many reasons for that, but I think I know one. We got good schools on the cheap for so long that we've forgotten or never really understood how much a good educational system costs.

Here's what I mean. Before women were given equal rights and equal access to jobs, there were really only two professions open to them: nursing and teaching. So the best and brightest became nurses and teachers.

The good news for the rest of us was we got good health care and good schools, and it didn't cost much. Since they couldn't work elsewhere, nurses and teachers were willing to work for very low wages. But when higher-salary jobs opened up for women, many women took them. And when they did, it created a crisis in nursing care, and our schools got worse. So why are we surprised?

Testing and accountability and all the things Congress and the president are debating to improve the schools are nice, but it's all small stuff; problem solving around the edges.

Good schools are the product of good teaching. Until we pay our teachers competitive wages, our schools won't change much.

—*May 6, 2001*

Vouchers

When the Supreme Court decided last week that school vouchers were constitutional, that it was legal for parents whose kids were stuck in bad schools to receive tax credits or government subsidies to send them to private schools, I was glad.

I went to public schools and am proud of it, and there was a time when I was against the whole concept of school vouchers, because I thought they would destroy the school system.

And to me, schools were always more than places our kids learned to read. They provided one of those common experiences, like the old draft army, that tied us together as a nation.

But I came to understand that the common experience of my generation is not the common experience of today's. In too many places, public schooling is an experience shared only by the poor, and too often, they are not even learning to read.

The clincher for me was this: there is a fine group in Washington called the I Have a Dream Foundation, which helps needy students. From them, I learned that a child can be placed in a good, safe private school for tuition that is considerably less than what the District of Columbia spends per child on students in its system.

Now, how can that be, that a small private school can educate a child for less money than a public school and do it in smaller, cleaner and safer classes? I don't know, but no parent, rich or poor, should have to put up with that.

That is why I believe we should begin pilot programs to test vouchers and any number of other innovative concepts, and the District of Columbia would be a fine place to start. Because what we're doing is not working. We need to find out what does.

—June 30, 2002

It was later explained to me that private schools can be operated cheaper than public schools because they don't have to pay for teaching students with special needs. I take the point, but our public schools are in such terrible shape in so many places, I still believe at least a voucher pilot program in selected areas is worth trying.

Listening in the Dark

O ne rainy night last week we were visiting some friends, and after dinner the lights went out. We figured it was just the weather and they'd come back on soon, so we just kept talking in the dark and listening to the rain.

Well, the lights never came back, but here's the surprising part: it didn't ruin the evening. It made it better. It reminded all of us of when we were children, before television, before air-conditioning, when families went to the front porch after dinner to cool off. We all remembered sitting in the dark for hours, talking, looking at the stars, hearing things the grown-ups didn't know we heard because they thought we had nodded off.

Today we live in the Information Age, but we're so bombarded with so much information from all sides now, from the television, the radio, the Internet, it all becomes a distraction.

Sitting in the dark the other night, it was as if we were freed from all of that. The conversation got better because our imaginations came into play, and we could pause from time to time just to listen to the rain.

I must also confess the discovery of another secret delight: when it's dark, you can close your eyes at any point in the conversation without offending anyone.

Very relaxing.

—June 24, 2001

Unreality

———

With a few days off over the holidays, I've been seeing the promos for the new summer reality shows and it's given me an idea.

As I understand it, these shows revolve around putting people in embarrassing situations and then watching them try to squirm out of it.

Points seem to go to the most devious, the ones who are willing to come up with the most ingenious ways to undercut their companions.

To the schemers go the spoils. Well, maybe I had too much Fourth of July, but I had a thought for another kind of story line.

What if there were a program that stressed teamwork instead of double-dealing, a program where you somehow got points for putting the common good ahead of personal ambition?

Now I know it sounds crazy, but I keep thinking that whatever gets done in this country, from little things like raising money to buy uniforms for the school baseball team, to big things like winning World War II, gets done because people work together.

Americans have always admired those who inspired us to be more than we thought we could be, not those who schemed to take advantage of our weaknesses and sell us out.

We mark George Washington's birthday not Benedict Arnold's. Now isn't that a story that still has some appeal?

We could even call it counterprogramming.

—July 8, 2001

To Know More

———

J ohn Adams loved to read and once said to his son, John Quincy, "You will never be lonely with a poet in your pocket."

I'm beginning to understand what he meant. I began David McCullough's splendid biography of Adams the week before July 4, and I finished it last week. And I feel suddenly as though I've lost a friend who has been with me all summer.

Maybe my age is showing, but the part I liked best was when Adams and Thomas Jefferson grew old, because it seemed to me they spent those years as people ought to—not trying to be young again, not making pests of themselves telling others what to do, but by forgiving their enemies, in their case, each other, by reading, maintaining contact with their friends and family and reflecting on their own lives and trying to learn from that.

The point of their later years was not to do more. They knew they had been part of something much larger than themselves, and they clearly enjoyed sharing the memories of it. No, their aim in those later years was to know more.

Jefferson, well into his eighties, and Adams, into his nineties, were never satisfied that they knew enough. And they kept trying until the end to learn more.

For the country they founded, we owe them everything. But we can also thank them for showing us a fine way to arrange our lives.

I'm going to miss them both.

—August 19, 2001

The Scandal and
the Church

———

As an admirer of the Catholic Church, I ask this question in sadness and in dismay, but it must be asked. Why are church leaders trying to make this latest scandal so complicated? It isn't.

The rules of the Catholic Church—celibacy, should priests marry, should women be barred from the priesthood—that's not my business. That's the business of Catholics, and it can be as theologically nuanced as they care to make it.

But protecting children from sexual predators is everyone's business, and it's not at all complicated. It is wrong and must be stopped. It requires no further study, no blue-ribbon commissions, no convoluted explanations. A few simple sentences will do just fine.

Anyone who harms a child should be removed from the Church and reported to the police. Anyone who harmed a child in the past should be removed from the Church and reported to the police. Anyone who knows of anyone who has harmed a child and tried to cover it up should be removed from the Church and reported to the police. Period.

When reform requires long explanations, it usually isn't reform, it's an excuse. There is a fine set of guidelines already available for those who will decide Church policy: the Ten Commandments, not just guidelines for content, but for style as well.

Short, simple, easy-to-understand sentences. That's what we need here.

—April 28, 2002

*News item: The Alabama Supreme Court ordered
a lower-court judge to remove a stone monument
containing the Ten Commandments from an
Alabama courthouse lobby.*

The Ten Commandments

As I watched the commotion over the Ten Commandments at the Alabama Supreme Court last week, the thought that kept running through my mind was this: What if Judge Moore had insisted on placing a large statue of the Buddha in the lobby, or perhaps a tribute to Mohammed, the founder of Islam? That's not so far-fetched, you know. There are more Muslims in America than Episcopalians, and a sizable Buddhist population, too. It's conceivable that one day a Muslim will be elected to a U.S. court. Would Judge Moore's supporters expect a Muslim-American judge to keep his religion a personal matter or would they want him to use his position to promote Islam?

I don't question their sincerity or their piety, but I hope they've begun to think about that, because Islam, like Judaism and Christianity, has been the guiding light now for millions of our citizens. Someone once said that any religion that needs the help of the state is not a very powerful religion. To suggest that these great religions, which have survived for thousands of years, somehow need or require the state government of Alabama to promote them is not only questionable, it borders on the blasphemous.

The true place of honor for the Ten Commandments is not a state courthouse, but the churches and synagogues of America. An even better place is deep inside our hearts. To place them otherwise is not to honor but to trivialize them.

—August 31, 2003

In English Only?

In the ongoing effort to make our national debate about all the wrong things, we may have reached a milestone with the controversy over whether it's all right for the National Anthem to be sung in Spanish.

The blogs went nuts about it, of course—going nuts is their natural state. Talk radio saw danger ahead—cover the children's ears.

I'm with them on insisting that everyone who wants to be a citizen should learn English. In an increasingly diverse country, common experiences have become rarer and rarer, and our language is one of the few things we all share. There is strength in that.

But the anthem in English only? I don't get it.

It made me proud to be an American when they tore down the Berlin Wall as "We Shall Overcome"—an American spiritual—played on the young people's boom boxes. And who among us can forget how we felt when those brave Chinese students brought a papier-mâché Statue of Liberty into Tiananmen Square?

When people take our symbols of freedom as their own, it doesn't weaken our values, it affirms they are universal. That makes us stronger, not weaker.

So I hope our anthem will be sung one day in a hundred languages, and I am not worried that translating it will somehow dilute its message. Translation hasn't seemed to hurt the Bible.

And since I speak neither Hebrew nor Greek, I'm glad they went to the trouble on that one. Otherwise, I might have missed the whole thing.

—*May 7, 2006*

Bonds was among the first to be suspected of steroid use,
but as we would learn later in 2007 when
the investigation of steroid usage was released,
he was far from the only one.

Barry Bonds Is No Hero

Americans love our sports, and we love our sports stars. And we love to keep score: who got the most hits; who ran the fastest mile; who ate the most hot dogs, for that matter.

Yet when Barry Bonds breaks the most famous record of all in the next week or so—Hank Aaron's home run record that has stood for more than three decades—many Americans won't cheer at all. They'll wish he hadn't been the one who did it.

Bonds is booed every place he plays except his home park in San Francisco. First, because he is widely believed to be a cheat who used illegal drugs to increase his strength. Second because he is a self-centered, all-around jerk who sees no responsibility to the fans who pay his enormous salary.

It's too bad, really. We want our heroes to be good guys, but maybe we need jerks like Bonds from time to time to remind us what real heroes are—and they are not just people who have mastered a difficult physical feat.

For sure, hitting home runs is hard to do. But so is standing on your thumb, which hardly qualifies thumb-standers to be heroes.

We admired Hank Aaron for hitting the home runs, but what made him an inspiration to others was the way he overcame adversity in order to set that record. The homers were just part of his greatness.

Real heroes are not just athletes. In fact, most of them are not: the firemen who gave their lives to save the innocent on 9/11; the soldiers who go into the streets of Baghdad day after day; parents who adopt handicapped children.

Heroes are those who set the examples we teach our kids to follow.

Barry Bonds is no hero. He is just a guy who hits home runs. Who would want a kid to be like him?

—*July 22, 2007*

Five months after breaking the home run record,
Barry Bonds was indicted for lying to a grand jury
about his alleged use of illegal drugs, and within days,
investigators released a report alleging that
many others had used the drugs as well.

A Very Bad Habit

When I was a kid, all I wanted to be was a ballplayer.

We didn't have coaches back then until we got to high school. We learned the game from each other and from copying the major leaguers. We copied everything, from their swings to the way they walked.

Because they chewed tobacco, I chewed. It was part of the game.

My dream to be a ballplayer ended, but it left me with a heavy addiction to nicotine.

Years ago, I finally beat it, but it was probably the reason I have a disease called ulcerative colitis, and almost certainly the cause of my bladder cancer decades later.

I still take drugs to control the colitis. Surgery got the cancer.

But I can only thank the stars there were no steroids in my younger days.

My baseball dream ended when I hurt my arm in high school and it finally gave out during my first year of college ball.

Had I known of a magic potion that would have made me stronger and kept the dream alive, I would have been no more hesitant to try it than I had been to chew tobacco. If my heroes had done it, that was all I needed to know.

The baseball stars got their names in the paper last week, but we buried the lead to this story. Deep in the report, it said hundreds of thousands of kids—kids who have the same dream I had—are putting their lives at risk using this stuff.

Who do we blame for that? Where are they getting it? How can their parents and even coaches NOT know?

That's where the follow-up stories should begin.

—*December 16, 2007*

The e-mail in response was overwhelmingly favorable, but the reaction reminded me that you can never please all of the people any of the time. One blogger said my willingness to try tobacco because others used it was a partial explanation for the media's herd mentality.

*News item: The family of baseball great Ted Williams
announced he will not be buried. Instead, his body will
be frozen in the hope that science will one day find a
way to bring people back to life.*

The Sunset of Life

I am at the stage of life where I spend most of my time trying
to keep the list of things I can do longer than the list of things
I can't. And let me tell you, it requires a lot more maintenance
than it used to—walking on a treadmill, taking my various pills and
reading all those nutrition facts printed in that tiny type on pack-
aged food.

Which got me to wondering, is there anything positive
about becoming more mature, as it were? And in fact, I've decided
there is.

Growing older reduces the number of things we need to worry
about. For example, which brand of motorcycle is most likely to be
stolen? I heard on the radio there's a new study about that, but I no
longer need to know the answer. Nor do I need to know how old
Britney Spears really is or whether she's had some work done.

I no longer need to worry about whether tattoos are safe, or
the best place to get body parts pierced, or to find low-rider blue
jeans, or whatever happened to Monica Lewinsky, or whether Bill
Clinton wore boxers, briefs or jammies with feet on them. Actually,
I never wondered about that, but I no longer need to worry about
those who did.

No, moving toward the sunset of life brings a certain clarity, a winnowing out of what's important and what isn't. Probably the most important thing is finally realizing we no longer have to worry about being cool. Of course, we do have to worry about our kids having us frozen.

—*August 11, 2002*

We Are All Broken

I have some thoughts for this season of reflection that began with Passover and ends with Easter.

Last summer at the Aspen Ideas Festival, I interviewed a minister named T. D. Jakes. He is an African-American pastor of a Dallas megachurch of more than thirty thousand people. He said something that day I shall never forget.

He reminded us that no one is perfect, that we are all broken somewhere.

But he said that is not all bad. A key is broken in all the right places to fit a certain lock. When *that* key is placed in *that* lock, there is a quiet click. When we meet a person who is broken in the right places to accommodate *our* brokenness, there is a click.

It can happen in other ways: an introverted person hears that click when he finds a job that can only be done by a person who works well alone.

Whether it is a job, or a relationship or even faith, something clicks when we find the place that accommodates our uniqueness, or brokenness.

Some religions teach prayer—some call it meditation—but there is within each of us some mysterious, inner thing that tells us when something clicks—we don't know how or why, we just know.

We are all broken. But listening for that click can help us to unlock many doors. The voice is always there—we have only to listen.

—*April 8, 2007*

IX

HUMAN INTERESTS

L et me begin with a confession. Some stories don't get on television or in the newspapers because they are important. They make it because they are just good stories—interesting, amusing, weird, whatever—and like porn, you know 'em when you see 'em. In the interest of even fuller disclosure, I love 'em.

My early journalism teachers taught that a newspaper was comprised of what readers need to know and what they want to know, and serious papers put more emphasis on the need-to-know than the want-to-know. When those REALLY REALLY SERIOUS FOLKS say there is no room for anything but the REALLY REALLY SERIOUS NEWS in a serious paper or television broadcast, I note the New York Times has a crossword puzzle, which no one really needs but that most people like—including me. The last time I looked, no one accused the Times of being light reading.

During that year and a half I anchored the Evening News, I was always on the lookout for "end pieces," those little stories that brought a chuckle at the end of the broadcast. They would generate complaints from some viewers, to be sure. One viewer took angry exception when we showed airport security guards marching a mother duck and her ducklings through a metal detector.

"Surely," the viewer wrote, "you could have found more important news to tell us about."

Well, of course I could.

I could also have found more important news than some of those pictures of cute panda cubs we showed from time to time. Actually, I blame *the pandas on our producer Jim Murphy, who liked pandas as much as Walter Cronkite liked fires and Dan Rather liked hurricanes, but with all the bad news we had to report, we thought just one teeny story that made us all feel a little better about things wouldn't stain our hard-news reputations.*

I know one thing, those were the stories the people in the office would be talking about the next day.

No doubt I could also have found more important stories than the cell phone adventures I chronicled in 2005. I was late to the cell phone fad, but once I got one, I was hooked. Even so, I am still awed by how these little gadgets have changed our lives.

I remember walking into a New York restaurant and noticing three people at one table talking on cell phones and wondering: Were they talking to each other? ("Could you pass the salt?" "How's the swordfish?") Important? No more than Henry Kissinger becoming a sports announcer or the man who was arrested for stealing a snake, but I managed to write stories about all of those things and some even weirder ones, and you know what? I enjoyed them all. Here's a brief selection, but I warn you: they're not really important.

No Police

Here's a little news just for the people here in the District of Columbia, where the potholes go unfilled, city services shrink as municipal bills go unpaid, and where, a couple of weeks ago, the mayor, Marion Barry, returned from a spiritual retreat to more or less say his plan to better deal with all this was to stop smoking.

Well, D.C. residents, if it's any comfort, we are not alone. The town of Gregory, Texas, population 2,600, has just seen municipal services not only shrink, they've lost the entire police force. When town fathers fired the chief, the rest of the force, all two of them, quit, leaving the town with no police at all. And it's not that they weren't needed. Once they left, thieves broke into the empty police station and stole all of the town's crime-fighting equipment: bullet-proof vests, a shotgun, radios and some other stuff.

It's tough all over these days.

—June 9, 1996

That was a couple of mayors ago and things got better in the District. I forgot to check on Gregory, Texas, but I guess we would have heard by now if something bad had happened.

Good News

W ith all this seamy stuff this week, I decided to look for some good news; and, sure enough, there was some. In Bradenton, Florida, the billfold containing $78 that Alan Bradley lost thirty years ago was returned to him by the man who found it, a man named Ernie Pitt. Mr. Pitt said he had six small children back in those days, and when he found that $78, it was like a godsend, but he said he always felt bad about it, so he traced Bradley through the Florida Department of Motor Vehicles and returned the billfold and, along with it, an apology and $200.

It was also a good week for Sylvia Stayton, the California woman who was fined $500 for putting quarters in strangers' parking meters so they wouldn't get parking tickets. Well, a San Francisco radio station took up a collection and sent her four thousand quarters.

And the federal government has finally issued a regulation that makes some sense. Remember that six-year-old North Carolina preschooler who was suspended from school and told he couldn't go to the class ice cream party because he had kissed a little female classmate on the cheek? Well, the Department of Education has issued guidelines clearly stating that is not sexual harassment. That means if there is another such incident, local schools won't have to worry about losing their federal funds. That makes you feel so warm and fuzzy, you want to hug someone, but be careful who.

And this was also the week that Henry Kissinger learned he will realize a lifetime ambition to become a sportscaster, sort of. He'll be inducted into the American Sportscasters Association. Maybe we could hug him.

—*March 16, 1997*

I love happy endings.

Online and Off

In our continuing effort to keep you abreast of the latest trends, social movements and various complications of modern life, we have found something new to worry about. Computers are posing a danger to marriage

The *Washington Post* reports that a Florida woman lost custody of her children because a divorce-court judge said she was spending too much time on the computer, sometimes seventeen hours at a stretch.

The woman denied that she had neglected the kids. She said the only reason she stayed online for so long was because it was so difficult to get a connection.

So naturally, she hesitated to sign off. Besides, she argued, most of the time, she was just exchanging information about pets with online friends.

She did not lose everything. The judge gave the husband custody of the kids, but she gets to keep the computer and the fax.

Now that's a cyberspace-age kind of settlement.

—*January 4, 1998*

Working the Phones

———

We've been having problems with our home telephone. Sometimes it rings when people call; sometimes it doesn't. So my wife called the people who sold it to us. Three days later, they called back to say they'd be sending someone by in two weeks to check it out. Furious at that, she spent a morning calling other companies that sell telephones.

She listened to a lot of recordings. Two days later, a human finally called back to say another human would be by in two more days. But when he arrived, he said it wasn't the phone; it was the phone line.

So my wife started calling the phone company. The folks there promised help in two more days, and, sure enough, in three days, someone did drop by. He fiddled with some wires and said he thought that was the problem.

I told my wife this is what happens when companies downsize, when they reduce the workforce to drive up profits. "But," I told her, "that's one reason the economy is booming, so we should be proud."

She says it's more complicated than that, that technology is just changing so rapidly, companies can't train people fast enough to operate and repair it.

Whoever is right, it does raise some interesting questions. Can an economic boom last if half the country's on hold and the other half is standing in line because there's no one available to sell them the goods and services they're trying to buy?

Or worse, what good is new technology if no one can operate it?

Whatever the case, the good news is, our phone finally seems to be working, but we've got our fingers crossed.

—June 28, 1998

A Real Snake

M y mother grew up during the Depression and kept a close watch on her worldly possessions and advised her children to do the same.

If she told us once, she must have told us a hundred times: "People will steal anything that's not nailed down," which is why I am sure she is looking down from the good place this morning, nodding her head and saying, "See, what did I tell you?"

Because a story moved on the wire today that a man in Florida has been arrested for stealing snakes—snakes from a pet shop.

When police arrived on the scene, the man first denied all of it, but then a boa constrictor peeped out from under his shirt and something moved around in his pants pocket and it turned out to be a milk snake.

The man claimed he really wasn't trying to steal the snakes, he had simply noticed them, he said, slithering across the floor, and put them in his pocket to keep them from escaping. The judge did not believe him and sentenced him to two years of house arrest. My mother would be very pleased with that.

—August 22, 1999

Everyone Cheered

Two nice things happened last week. The first one involved a United Airlines flight bound from Washington to California. About halfway there, the pilot learned that a passenger's dog had been mistakenly placed in the plane's unheated forward cargo hold, where he was certain to freeze. The pilot notified the passenger, a man named Mike Bell, told him he couldn't be sure he could save the dog but would do his best, then flipped on the intercom and told the passengers he was going to make an emergency stop in Denver, quote, "for the best interest of the dog," end quote.

Well, here's the remarkable part of this story in this day of impatience and road rage. Not one passenger complained about the delay, and everyone cheered when the little dog was finally brought out of the cargo hold, wrapped in a blanket and placed in the seat next to his owner for the rest of the ride. That's how people used to act when we thought of each other as neighbors.

But more remarkable is what happened in a courtroom in Washington's Virginia suburbs this week. A deaf couple who had miscalculated their disability benefits were hauled into Judge Donald P. McDonagh's court by a landlord who wanted them evicted because they'd fallen $250 behind in their rent. When Judge McDonagh realized there was no other way out, he whipped out $250 in cash and said, quote, "I'll pay it. Case dismissed." Another neighborly act, to say the least.

Who knows? The way things are going, maybe it's the beginning of some kind of trend.

—*June 11, 2000*

It wasn't, but it was nice while it lasted.

And speaking of dogs, I couldn't resist noting the results of the Westminster Dog Show in 2008, even though this report clearly shows that bias in the media does exist.

Top Dog

W always watch the telecast of the Westminster Kennel Club Dog Show at our house, and when Uno the beagle took best in show I cheered out loud. My wife cried real tears of joy.

Beagles are the best dogs that ever were. I feel the same way about dogs that I do about food. I like my food to look like food. The meat in its place on the plate, the vegetables in theirs—not all stacked up like some cutesy piece of art. And, please, flowers belong in vases, not on my plate.

As for dogs, I like them to look like dogs, not some perfumed ball of fur that resembles a powder puff. You wouldn't paint a beagle's toenails or put ribbons in a beagle's fur.

We had three beagles at our house. Ralph, whose keen nose found the book satchel stuffed with beer that the boys hid in our garden the night of the first boy-girl party at our house. Old Ralph held his point until I removed it.

Then there was little Dixie, who gave a light bite to the diplomat from the Chinese embassy who strolled past our house one morning. It was just after Tiananmen Square; clearly, a brave act of political protest.

And there was sweet Betty. Such a shy little city dog. She didn't even like to go outside without a leash.

It took a hundred years, but America is a better place when beagles rule. Good dog, Uno.

—*February 17, 2008*

Coping with the Cell Phone Culture

This is another in our occasional comments on the cell phone culture.

I realized a long time ago that cell phones are not to communicate. They are the new cigarette, something to grab when we're nervous, but I have come to believe they are something more, a magic carpet that takes us from reality to a different place, like a child who reads *Harry Potter* or the drunk who believes he is invisible as in, "It's okay, honey. They'll never see us over here."

Cell phone users are transported to a place where they no longer see or hear the world around them. Unfortunately, in the world around them, where the rest of us are, we hear them. It's like standing on the corner when one of those cars that blare rap music stops for a light. Mercifully, the cars move on. These ego-phoniacs just keep on talking about things that are, one, boring, or, two, no one else's business.

In the Denver Admirals Club airport lounge early one morning last week, I listened for a full half hour as a woman explained confidential details of a business presentation, including her company's fallback positions. What would the other side have paid for what was being forced on me for free?

I'm not sure how the rest of us can combat this, but here is one thought. The next time an ego-phoniac shares a secret you don't want to hear, just join in the conversation, something like, "Why, that's a terrible idea," or, "Don't be such a gutless ninny. Stand up for yourself."

On second thought, that could be a good way to get hit in the mouth with a cell phone. Still, it might be worth the risk.

—July 24, 2005

Talking the Talk

I am convinced that when Judgment Day comes, half the people in line at the Pearly Gates will be talking on cell phones. Seeing those pictures last week of the woman who continued to talk on her cell phone while robbing a bank left me more convinced of that than ever.

And that got the people in our newsroom to wondering: Is there any place in American life where cell phones have not intruded? Apparently not.

One colleague heard a guy on a train fire someone by cell phone;

another became so annoyed by a loud cell-phoner that when he over-heard the guy give his phone number, my friend just wrote it down and called him. He had call-waiting, and when he answered, my friend told him to please shut up.

I once heard a guy in a men's room stall calling someone to ask for a date. I've always wondered how he explained the flushing sounds. "By the way, honey, I'm calling from Niagara Falls."

But my favorite phone story comes from a friend who was on a train sitting beside a woman in her sixties who had phoned her psychiatrist to complain about sexual pressure from her boyfriend, who kept waking her at three in the morning. It is beside the point, I know, but from what my friend could make out, the psychiatrist told her to start charging the guy rent.

If you would like to hear your favorite cell phone story on TV, just send it to me, but do us all a favor—*e-mail* us.

—*November 14, 2005*

Mind you, this one came long before Larry Craig.

Just Call on Me

I promise, no more cell phone stories for a while. But after my rant last week on cell phone bad manners, so many of you wrote in with your own horror stories that I want to share a few of them.

Would you believe a driving-school instructor talking on a phone while giving a lesson to a student driver? A viewer named Clyde saw it.

Jeanne from California saw a woman talking on a cell phone at a funeral.

Debbie swears a woman at her church took Communion while talking on a cell phone. Maybe she was talking to the Lord.

On a visit to Washington, Brent and his wife saw a beggar. As they approached, the beggar took a cell phone from his ear and asked if they could spare some change.

And at the Colosseum in Rome, Kurt and his wife saw a man dressed in the authentic costume of a Roman centurion talking on a cell phone. *Et tu*, Verizon?

To say the least, there were a lot of stories involving cell phone multitasking in restrooms. My favorite came from Charles, who heard someone in the next stall say, "Hello." Startled, he responded, "Hi." Which prompted the voice to say, "Any plans for tonight?"

That brought a quick, "Sorry, I'm busy," to which the voice next door responded, "I'll just have to call you back. Every time I ask you a question, the idiot in the next stall answers."

—*November 20, 2000*

Like all such things, I suppose we'll survive the changes that cell phones brought to our lifestyle. But I remain worried. Sooner or later, someone will decide cell phones are bad for our health. Sooner or later, someone decides that about everything, which means cell phone usage will be banned indoors. This means our sidewalks, already crowded by young women smokers, will become impassable, and cell phone users will be forced into the streets, where they will risk being run over by drivers using cell phones.

If it's not the phone, it's something else.

Staying in Touch
Too Much

D id you see that article in the *New York Times* about how college professors are having trouble getting their work done because they get so much e-mail from students?

E-mail has changed everything—walls are coming down. There is a new familiarity between students and teachers, the media and its readers and viewers, business and its customers, government and its citizens.

That's good news for the most part, but not for all parts. Student e-mailers have become so brash they no longer have qualms about ripping into a teacher's methods to justify bad grades. Or, as the *Times* told it, using a bad hangover as an excuse for missing class.

Which makes me wonder: Are we staying in touch *too* much? Have cell phones and e-mail become the crutches we never needed until we had them? Has the new familiarity given way to rudeness and stupidity?

Worse, is our new ability to communicate with almost everyone and to do it instantly causing us to lose our ability to reflect, to think before we speak?

Why would even a freshman believe getting drunk was an excuse for missing class? Or that you'd get a better grade by roasting the one who hands out the grades?

Venting may be good for mental health, but does not always equate with logic.

Maybe we should all turn off our phones and the BlackBerrys for a second and think about this: when Benjamin Franklin was in Europe negotiating terms to end our revolutionary war, six weeks would sometimes pass before he got instructions from home.

Yet he worked out a pretty good deal. Of course, he spent a lot of time practicing what seems a lost art—thinking.

—February 26, 2006

My heavens, has it come to this?

Sorry, Andy

Maybe I'm just getting old, but I think what the world needs is a better class of people making the news. Too many of these people who get attention these days just seem ridiculous. Yet they're the ones who make the papers and the TV. Like that guy who had himself suspended for months in a glass box over London Bridge. Was I supposed to care? Well, now it can be told; I didn't.

And that other guy who went over Niagara Falls without a barrel. Now that's quite a feat. A 180-foot drop straight down to a churning river with rocks all around. He said it was something he just always wanted to do. But here is my question. Should we have been upset if he had been killed? I suppose so. But to be honest—well, never mind.

And then there was that multimillion-dollar lawsuit that Liza Minnelli's estranged husband filed against her because he said she beat him up all the time. Something about she's strong as a bull when she's drinking vodka or some such. And can't you just imagine? It got big play in all the papers, and, yes, I was shocked to know that a wedding that had featured Michael Jackson as the best man and Liz Taylor as the matron of honor could end up going so bad. But, so far, I have had no trouble remaining unmoved. I know this is a character flaw, and I'm trying to work through it.

But here's the part that worries me. If people like this keep getting all the attention, I may wind up sounding like Andy Rooney.

—October 26, 2003

X

THE LIVES WE LED

I have a confession.

   The older I get, the more I enjoy the obituary page, especially the obits in the New York Times, *whose death notices set the standard for all of journalism.*

   No other section of the newspaper causes me to pause so many times and say to myself, "I didn't know that," or "I hadn't thought of that in just that way."

   Over the years on the occasions when I closed Face the Nation *with a few words on the death of someone, most of the time those words were based on information gleaned from the* Times.

   As I read through those commentaries, I also realized that in their own way the obituaries offer a guide to a meaningful life.

   I was reminded, as well, that it is not always the rich and powerful who make the difference in our lives, it might be a policeman or a circus high-wire artist or a photographer or a wacky actress or just an old pal who knew something about politics.

   It's all there in the obits.

The Obits

———

S omebody, I think it was Ronald Reagan, actually, once said he
liked to start the day by turning to the obituary page in the
newspaper because it was such a pleasure to discover his name was
not listed there.

Well, I've also reached the part of life where I check the obits
more closely than I once did. But when two friends recently told
me on separate occasions that the obituary page in the *New York
Times* had become their favorite part of the newspaper, it occurred
to me that we're attracted to obits for more than just a confirmation
that we're still alive. And I believe a part of that attraction has to do
with the way we define news. Walter Cronkite once observed that,
by nature, most news is bad or at least depressing. "It's news in the
neighborhood when someone's cat runs off," he said. "All the cats
and dogs that stayed home are not news."

That's why so much of a newspaper or a television newscast is
filled with accounts of things that have gone wrong—policies that
collapsed, plans that backfired, planes that crashed, hypocrisy that's
been laid bare and people whose bad side got the best of them. It is
not until we get to the obituary page, especially the *Times*'s obituary
page, which is so well written and researched, that we find stories
about those who actually accomplished something—people who
invented things or found cures for diseases or wrote books that mattered, who were simply good bosses or conscientious workers or loving mothers and fathers.

The obituaries remind us that there's a lot more going on in the

world than just the news. So if you're feeling low, here's a summer
reading tip: check the obit page and have a nice day.

—*August 27, 1995*

Angel Wallenda

I t was crowded off the front pages and the newscasts by what may
have seemed to be more important news this week, but deep in
the pages of the *New York Times*, there was a wonderful story about
a wonderful life that bears repeating.

It was an account of the very short life of Angel Wallenda, who
had married into the famous circus family at the age of seventeen
after surviving a nightmare childhood in which she was beaten and
starved and finally overcame drugs.

When her husband-to-be found her scooping ice cream in a
shopping mall and invited her to join the family high-wire act, she
accepted without hesitation because she said it sounded like a great
adventure.

But shortly after she began her training, she developed cancer.
Eventually, her right leg was amputated below the knee, parts of
her lung were removed, but she continued training and eventually walked the high wire on an artificial limb. She said she did it,
"Because when I'm way up there in the sky walking on a thin line
with a fake leg, people look up at me and really pay attention. They
see I'm using everything I've got to live my life the best way I can.
It makes them think about themselves, and some of them see how
much better they could live their own lives. Maybe that is my main
purpose for being here."

Angel Wallenda was just twenty-eight when the cancer finally got her this week. Go in any bookstore these days and you'll find shelves filled with books about whether angels really exist.

Well, we know there's at least one, don't we?

—*May 5, 1996*

Scott Lewis

On Friday, I saw a long line of police cars and firefighting equipment moving up one of Washington's busiest thoroughfares, and I realized that I had happened on the funeral procession for Scott Lewis, a twenty-eight-year-old policeman in the District of Columbia who had been killed in the line of duty.

Seeing that long line of mourners made me think of the questions we usually ask in times of tragedy: Why do such things happen and what do they mean?

If the newspapers had it right, this is what happened. A man with a gun walked up to Scott Lewis and his partner and shot Lewis in the head and that was the end of the life of Scott Lewis, a fine young person by all accounts, with two years on the police force.

The saddest part of this story is that is all there is to it. There was no warning, no reason, no explanation. The gunman's motivation went to the grave with him because Lewis's partner killed him.

Well, perhaps we can never know why such things happen, but we can think about what they mean. And one thing this story means is that police officers are put in such situations every day.

Few of us go to work wondering if we'll be killed. But that is part of the job description for every police officer.

For all the talk about bad cops these days, this story also reminds us that most of the police are not like that. They are decent, brave people, like young Scott Lewis, who are willing to put themselves in dangerous situations because it's simply what they signed on to do.

—October 15, 1995

Diana

Perhaps she was the most famous person in the world. People came to know her in the beginning as a glamorous character in a fairy tale, the beautiful young woman who found her handsome prince and was married in a dream-come-true wedding, the kind that is supposed to end with "and they lived happily ever after."

But, of course, it did not end that way, because fairy tales are fairy tales and life is life, and in the end the fairy tale became a soap opera about life in the fast lane, a lane where Diana died.

In a celebrity-driven media culture, many loved her for trying to use her celebrity for good causes.

Others admired her not so much for what she had done but for what had been done to her as a woman wronged.

Still others adored her simply because she was famous and glamorous.

Not so long ago, she described Dodi Fayed, the new man in her life, as "the man who will take me out of one world and into another." But that could not be. For commoner or king, for good or the bad, the only certainty about life is death at a time and in circumstances over which we have no control.

In the novel *Lonesome Dove*, Gus McCrae is asked to say a few words as a young cowboy is being buried, and the only thing he can think to say is that, "Life is short, and for some it is shorter than others." It's a reminder of the pointlessness of trying to understand death and a recognition that life is precious and what really matters is how we live it.

—August 31, 1997

James Michener

When the news of James Michener's death at the age of ninety came over the wires this week, I remembered an early morning back in the seventies when I was to interview him on the *CBS Morning News*. He had come to talk about a book he'd just written, but Iran was coming apart and unedited pictures of Muslim demonstrations were coming in over the satellite. We wanted to put the pictures on the air immediately, and so I asked if he would be willing to forgo an interview and instead just watch the pictures with me and comment on them as we shared them with our viewers.

There was not a moment of hesitation. "Oh, yes," he said, "much more interesting," adding, "I want to see those pictures, too."

James Michener was first and foremost a great reporter, and that long-ago morning helped me to understand why. Great reporters have two common traits: curiosity and the love of a good story.

Michener, into his nineties, was curious about everything, so much so that he never let himself get in the way of a good story. Instead, his curiosity drove him to where the story was and to stay there until he knew more about it than anyone else and could tell it in an entertaining way.

His books reflected that. Michener never got a chance to sell his book on that long-ago morning news, but he didn't need to. They sold themselves, 75 million at last count, and they are still counting.

—*October 19, 1997*

Dave Powers

I saw in the *New York Times* that Dave Powers, a legendary character, longtime friend and aide to President Kennedy, died last week at the age of eighty-five.

The paper said that they met one night when a young Jack Kennedy knocked on the door of Powers's sister's house in the Charlestown section of Boston, announced he was running for Congress and asked Powers for help. Powers did, and he proved invaluable. He knew everyone in the neighborhood. He had known most of them since the days he was the neighborhood newsboy. The rest he knew from church, where he ushered at five services every Sunday.

I never met Powers, but I felt I knew him because there was a Dave Powers around every campaign I ever saw growing up; the guy who always knew the old neighborhood, knew who counted and who didn't, what mattered to the people there and what didn't. There aren't many of them around anymore. They were pushed aside years ago by the people who turned politics into a business.

These days, a politician hires a professional pollster to tell him what the community is thinking, a professional consultant to tell him what to think.

In today's politics, you have to wonder if Kennedy and Powers would have even met. Candidates can reach so many more people through television ads, they no longer consider it cost-effective to go door-to-door. I guess it marks me as an old coot, but I thought it worked better when the politicians leaned more on the guys who knew the old neighborhood.

—*March 29, 1998*

Madeline Kahn

Madeline Kahn, the actress, died last week. She was just fifty-seven, and it was cancer. I knew her only by her work, but I'm going to miss her because she was so funny. And in a funny way, as artists sometimes do, she became a part of my life.

It began way back when Jimmy Carter was president and I was sent out to watch him vacation on the Salmon River in Idaho. Now going on vacation is fun, but watching someone vacation is pretty boring. So with nothing else to do, all of us reporters assigned to watch the Carters watched movies at night. This was no mean feat in the middle of nowhere, and even harder because we had no projector and only one movie, *Blazing Saddles*, starring Madeline Kahn, among others.

This was long before you could rent movies at the video store, but our tape editor, Phil Gillespie, found a way. He somehow transferred the film to videotape, so we could watch the movie on the editing equipment that we used to make our TV reports.

We watched it every night. Finally, we edited the entire movie down to a twelve-minute version that contained only the movie's punch lines. I have since forgotten all the jokes, but I will never forget the punch lines, especially when Madeline Kahn, in her Elmer Fudd accent, exclaimed, "It's twue. It's twue. It's weawy twue."

It became our watchword that summer, our secret code. We said it over and over, and outsiders were puzzled when we would break into gales of laughter.

So thank you, Madeline Kahn, for the laughs and even more for the memories. Every time I saw you on television, it reminded me of that summer and how much fun it is to be a reporter, even on a dull assignment.

—December 5, 1999

Russell Long

R ussell Long, who knew a lot about human nature, said most people's feelings about taxes could be summed up this way: Don't tax him, don't tax me, tax that fellow behind the tree.

Long served thirty-five years as the senator from Louisiana and probably knew more about, and had more influence over, the tax code than any senator before or since. He died this weekend as Congress was mired in yet another impenetrable gridlock over cutting taxes, an argument that has fiscal conservatives saying deficits don't count, traditional big-spender Democrats saying they do, and moderate Republicans saying the way to break the deadlock and give the president the tax cut he wants is to raise taxes in two dozen other areas.

Excuse me, but this sounds more like politics than economic policy, and I wondered how Russell Long would have felt.

He always had the ability to see beyond the battle of the moment. He knew the people at the bottom could always use a little help at tax time, but he also knew you couldn't put all the taxes on business.

You can't have capitalism, he said, without capital. Long had a way of seeing the big picture and finding a way to work out something that both sides could accept. Too many of today's fund-raiser politicians can't see beyond the positions of their campaign contributors, which is why real compromise is so rare now and the kind of morass where Congress finds itself is so common.

No politician did more for his state than Russell Long, but occasionally he went against public opinion, as when he voted for the Panama Canal treaty. Because, he said, a politician's first obligation was not to please his constituents, but to give them his best judgment. That's a philosophy we don't hear much anymore.

—*May 11, 2003*

Johnny Cash

Johnny Cash died this week after a hard life.

He had picked cotton before he picked a guitar, but he never forgot that and you could see that in his face and hear it in his songs.

In 1989, my first book had just come out and I was in New York signing some copies of it at a bookstore and up walked Johnny Cash. He had an armload of books, held up mine and in that unique voice said, "I'll buy this if you sign it for me."

Of course I did. I was thrilled. I'd never met him, but we had a fine talk about news and books.

He was a voracious reader, and as other customers happened by, he chatted with them, too—not a star talking to fans, just one book browser chatting with others.

He was plagued by demons all his life, but he conquered them and made it to the top. But unlike so many who do that, once there, he did not conclude he had done it all alone or that if he could, there was no excuse for those who could not.

No, he just knew life was hard, and we knew that he knew. That's why he gave hope to anyone who ever went through a hard time.

He told us to take life as it comes. If he could get through it, we thought maybe we could, too.

I just liked him because what you saw on TV was what you saw when the cameras turned away.

That's not always the way it is. I know because I know a lot of people on TV.

—September 14, 2003

Eddie Adams

You may have seen in the paper that the great Associated Press photographer Eddie Adams died. He was seventy-one.

It was Lou Gehrig's disease.

Eddie won the Pulitzer for a picture he took in Vietnam of a South Vietnamese colonel executing a Viet Cong agent, a picture he came to hate after he learned the agent had killed the colonel's family.

When I was a young newspaper reporter in Vietnam, Eddie and I often traveled together and we had a deal. He taught me how to cover a war and take pictures.

In return, I caught cutlines for him. That is, I took down the names of the people he photographed and wrote captions for his pictures.

He was as brave a guy as I ever knew, and traveling with him had its moments. Once, when a Buddhist riot broke out and the American government didn't want us to cover it, an American MP pulled his pistol and told us to come no farther.

Eddie raised his camera and said, "Okay, you pulled that pistol. Now just use it." The problem was the MP was aiming at me, not at Eddie.

We talked our way out of it, and later Eddie just laughed and said he was pretty sure the guy was just bluffing.

Eddie's friend Pete Hamill wrote this week that whenever he saw Eddie after the war, Eddie would always remark on what a glorious day it was.

And so he did. Because long after the rhetoric is spent, long after the generals' explanations and the politicians' debates over who was right and who was wrong have ended, what those who are sent to our wars and those who have seen the killing up close always remember first is that they survived to see another day.

Eddie Adams, what a guy.

—September 26, 2004

Pope John Paul II

———

You didn't have to be Catholic to be moved by the events of these past days. You didn't even have to be religious.

Just seeing the millions gathered in Rome and realizing it was the largest spontaneous gathering of humans in the whole history of the world was enough to take your breath away.

To me, the most moving scenes of all were seeing the old Pope, so near death, insisting that he be brought to the window to bless the crowds one more time.

It was not just his love but his sense of duty to those he led that impressed me. I kept thinking about that as the week unfolded and we saw another spectacle—preparations for the wedding of Prince

Charles, a man who gets paid for doing nothing yet seems put upon because he has to do it...nothing, that is.

We read of his exasperation that the wedding had to be put off a day in deference to the Pope's funeral, and we watched him sneer at photographers who asked him to pose for some pre-wedding pictures with his sons.

My heavens, what imposition will he next have to endure, a photo with his mom?

This was a week for prayer, but I must admit one of mine was to give thanks that I was born in a country whose founders were among the first to recognize the silliness of the whole idea of royalty and made sure we would never have to fool with it.

—April 17, 2005

Peter Jennings

In an awful week, the one thing that made a lot of people I know feel a little better was, of all things, a funeral, or to be more accurate, a memorial service for my friend Peter Jennings, because it wasn't the usual memorial service.

Peter's wife, Kayce, saw to it that the 2,200 people who came to Carnegie Hall were treated to a great show. And from the Royal Canadian Mountie Honor Guard, to the New York Police Department bagpiper who started it, to Yo-Yo Ma and Wynton Marsalis and the Gates of Praise Choir that brought us all to our feet at the end, it was just that, a wonderful show.

It made us all think of Peter because he loved a good show. And in the ultimate sign of respect in today's modern world, the crowd actually turned off their cell phones and listened. I only heard one ringing. And it made me grin because I know Peter would have noticed.

And there was another rarity. The people who gave the eulogies passed up the chance to talk about themselves and actually talked about Peter. And there were none of the usual bromides about Peter's commitment to a free press. With Peter, that was a given. Instead the speeches were very personal. His friends talked about his work with the homeless, his fondness for kids, and his relationship with his own son and daughter. His son Chris said, "There is no way to express how much I miss my father. Each day is, above all, a day without him."

Peter rose to the top of his profession and won every prize you can win. But as I heard that young man speak, I wondered if anything Peter had ever achieved would have made him prouder than to hear his son say those words. I think not. And that is what made Peter Jennings worth knowing. I'm proud I did.

—September 25, 2005

Paul Tibbets

On August 6, 1945, a pilot named Paul Tibbets climbed into a plane named for his mother and flew to Japan on what would be one of the most famous flights in aviation history. The plane was the *Enola Gay*, and on board was the first atomic bomb ever used in war, which would be dropped directly over city hall in a place called Hiroshima.

In an instant, more than one hundred thousand people were killed or wounded. Many were vaporized. More would die from radiation poisoning.

The bomb, and another dropped at Nagasaki, brought an end to the war. And the coming of atomic power marked a turning point in the twentieth century.

Tibbets became a national hero, and he expressed no regrets, then or later. He felt the bomb had saved more lives than would have been lost had the war gone on. But as the years passed, the bombing became so controversial that he asked that he be cremated when he died for fear protesters would deface a gravestone.

Yet when he died last week, his passing drew little comment. His obituary was buried deep inside the major newspapers, and TV gave his passing less coverage than the death of singer Robert Goulet.

In a nation where the median age is now thirty-five, the name Paul Tibbets meant nothing to many.

Not so for those of a certain age. For us, it is a somber reminder that the war we can still remember is getting to be a long time ago.

—November 4, 2007

William F. Buckley

The passing last week of William F. Buckley, the founder of the modern American Conservative movement, brought many tributes.

For me, it brought back a fond memory of the one time I met Buckley and what I learned from him that day.

We were not much alike. He was New York's Upper East Side. I am Fort Worth's lower North Side.

By college, he knew he was a Conservative. I still can't figure out what I am. As I have grown older, "confused" is one word that has been suggested.

Once, long ago, we were on a seminar panel assembled by broadcasting legend Fred Friendly. I was a young reporter and he was, well, William F. Buckley.

He said something. I took immediate and sharp exception. Suddenly I realized I had picked a fight with one of America's keenest intellects—maybe the best debater in America. In a word, I was terrified. I was certain he would shred my argument to pieces, and me along with it.

But he let me down gently. He made his point but with that twinkle in the eye that was so much a part of him, he actually left the impression my point may have been worth making.

He was interested in ideas, not in tearing down those who didn't see it his way on some particular point. He delighted in taking on people his own size, but he saw no need that day to embarrass some kid who was just starting out.

I'm sure he never gave the moment another thought, but I never forgot it.

—March 2, 2008

XI

THE UNTHINKABLE

We know what a dollar is, or even five hundred dollars, but a billion dollars is beyond our imagination, so when we read that a congressman hid ninety thousand dollars in his home freezer, it triggers more outrage than reading that a government agency wasted billions. We've seen a suitcase filled with thousands of dollars on television cop shows. No one ever saw a stack of bills that came to a billion, so we can't really imagine how much money that is.

So it was when 9/11 happened. It was not beyond our intelligence-gathering capability, it was simply beyond our imagination, as my friend and New York Times columnist Tom Friedman would later observe.

During the half century I have covered the news, I have come to appreciate the indestructibility of the human spirit, but I have also come to recognize the depths of inhumanity and the capacity for cruelty that rest deep within humankind.

I believe there is such a thing as evil; we may not know from where it comes, but it is there and it is real.

How else to explain so many of the events that have happened even in the short periods of our lifetimes?

We ask what has been asked so many times over thousands of years, "Why do bad things happen to good people?" Yet we are no closer to an answer than the first human who asked. Nor has the capacity or willingness to invoke horror on others been reduced over time.

The unspeakable atrocities of the Nazis did not happen during some long-ago time and in some faraway place. They happened during our time.

During the half century I have been a reporter, I have covered many events for which I had no answer, from the assassination of a young president to the cruelties of war and, of course, 9/11. But during none of those stories did I feel the presence of evil in the way I felt it that day in 1975 when I went to a Nazi death camp with President Gerald Ford.

I begin this chapter with the story I wrote that day for CBS Radio.

A Grayness Within Grayness

There is a special flag that flies over Auschwitz now. It is a flag of blue-and-white stripes—that is because the prisoners who were kept here wore blue-and-white-striped uniforms. There is a red triangle at the left side of the flag; that is because on each prisoner's shirt pocket there was a triangle of some color—more red triangles than any other kind, because the color red denoted political prisoners.

When President Ford came here yesterday, the flag billowed in a soft breeze, but the breeze did not carry the stench that hung over this place just a little over thirty years ago, the stench that came from the ovens.

Now, behind the high barbed-wire fences that have surrounded that awful place since the Nazis built it in 1940, there stands not far from where the ovens were a memorial to the ones who never left there.

At the base of that monument, the president laid a wreath yesterday. It was placed not far from the nineteen stone tablets that are arranged along the monument base, to explain in nineteen languages what it is that happened there in one period of less than five years, that four million people, some of them old, most of them sick, many of them children, were murdered in cold blood.

At a small museum not far from the memorial and inside the barracks and the ruins of the crematoriums, they sell little guidebooks that tell more of this place in the words of those who were held here and those who held them here.

Here are some of the things that the book says.

From the diary of Heinrich Himmler, who ran the Gestapo—"The Führer has ordered that the Jewish question be settled once and for all—I have earmarked Auschwitz for this purpose because it is of good position as regards communication and because the area can be easily isolated and camouflaged."

From the diary of the camp commandant, Rudolf Hess—"About four thousand Gypsys were left in Auschwitz by August 1944, and these had to go to the gas chamber. It was not easy to drive them to the gas chamber."

From a Nazi letter in 1942—"The Slovak government pays five hundred marks for every extradicted Jew and also covers the cost of transportation."

From Hess again—"Toward the end of the summer we started to burn bodies—at first on wood pyres, burning some 2,000 corpses."

Again from Hess—"I had to build the camps at Birkenau with the help of the prisoners themselves. The officers who escorted them said they were the best of the lot but they were dying off due to general exhaustion and the slightest illnesses."

From a woman prisoner—"We saw the camp for the first time in daylight. We saw a grayness within grayness. As far as the eye could see we saw barracks and barbed wire broken here and there by tall towers with machine guns."

From the medical log of Dr. Clauberg—"Should the investigations conducted by myself continue as expected, and I foresee no obstacles, then in the nearest future I hope to be able to say that a properly trained surgeon, with perhaps ten medical assistants, will be in position to sterilize several hundred or even one thousand persons in the course of one day."

From a man who had been held here as a boy—"We were separated from our parents, and though we knew the exact day on which they were to be gassed, not one among us was able to weep anymore."

From the diary of Bertholt E., another ex-prisoner—"During the selection of children, the S.S. men had placed a rod at the height of 1.2 meters. Children who had passed under the rod would be gassed. Small children, knowing only too well what was awaiting them, tried hard to push out their necks when passing under the rod."

From Hess as the end approached—"In the confines of my cell I have come to the realization that I have committed atrocious crimes."

—*July 30, 1975*

Oklahoma City

At the White House this morning, the president and Mrs. Clinton planted a tree in memory of the children who died in Oklahoma City. Later today, the first family will participate in a memorial service for all the victims in Oklahoma City.

As all of us watched these terrible events on television this week, we were reminded that there is something called evil in the world, that it is as real as the sun above us and the earth below us, and that it is not always visited upon us by those who live in a different place.

We were also reminded there is goodness, and in the wake of this monstrous act, we saw how real that can be. In a nation that has sometimes seemed indifferent, lately, to its neighbors, Oklahoma City's children became all our children. At a time when government bureaucrats are demonized, we saw a magnificently coordinated effort, federal, state and local officials and just plain neighbors working to comfort the victims and track down the killers; firemen and policemen who refused to go home when their shifts were over; doctors who gave no thought to personal safety.

The historian Will Durant once wrote that barbarism, like the jungle, does not die out, but only retreats behind barriers that civilization has thrown up against it and waits there, always to reclaim that to which civilization has temporarily laid claim.

The barriers against barbarism are love, compassion, hard work, intelligence and courage, and even through the rubble of this awful week in Oklahoma City, we saw them reinforced.

In an awful week, we also saw America at its best.

—*April 23, 1995*

*On August 3, 1996, a plane carrying Commerce
Secretary Ron Brown and thirty-two others
crashed during a violent rainstorm in Croatia.
All thirty-two aboard were killed.*

A Very Small Place

Washington is a place that usually has all the answers because it's a place that deals in the abstract. We hold debates of great passion about poverty, based not on experiences with the poor but on what we refer to as shocking statistics about poverty. We debate Bosnian terrorism, not because we have faced it firsthand but because we have seen shocking pictures on television.

But official Washington is a very small place, and last week was no different. The horrible pictures we saw on television were not about strangers we had never met; they were about Washington.

Nearly everyone in official Washington knew someone on Ron Brown's plane, or knew their wife, or worked with their husband, or had kids who went to school with their kids or in several cases had been on the same plane themselves the week before.

As Ann Devroy and Kevin Merida wrote in the *Washington Post* the day after the tragedy: "The men and women of official Washington paused from the business of government yesterday to pray and hug and cry and comfort one another."

The city that has all the answers was no longer dealing with the abstract. Suddenly, it was confronted with a situation whose reason for happening seemed beyond human comprehension. Perhaps at such a time, and especially in this week when Jews remember the Passover and Christians celebrate Easter, it is good to remember the great truth that both religions share: that by looking deep within ourselves, we may find strength that goes far beyond ourselves.

—April 7, 1996

Falling to Earth

When they told Harry Truman that Franklin Roosevelt had died, Truman said he felt as if the sun and the moon and the stars had fallen from the sky.

I guess a lot of us felt that way yesterday when we saw those television pictures of the shuttle breaking up and the pieces falling back to Earth.

I guess the first thought a lot of you had was the same one I had: Was this the work of terrorists?

They say it wasn't, that it all happened too far up in the sky, but it is a sign of our times that when anything untoward happens, our first thought is: Did terrorists do it? Terrorists have become so much a part of our lives, we are surprised when they are not the cause of terrible things.

Space travel, on the other hand, has gone so well for so long that it has become routine. We take it for granted.

It is anything but routine.

We are, after all, the first people who have lived on this planet who have found a way to travel beyond it, which may be the most remarkable achievement of our generation.

The foundation of America's strength has always been the courage of its people to explore the unknown, to cross the river that has not been crossed, to go to the other side of the mountain.

The men and women who died yesterday were the latest in a long line of Americans who have had the courage to lead us to the next frontier.

So even as the possibility of war looms, we must pause to remember their courage and the courage of those who came before.

The stars did not fall yesterday, but we are ever closer to them.

—February 2, 2003

9/11

Americans came together this week as they have not come together since World War II. You could see it and feel it and not just in the calls for retaliation. I noticed it first as I was driving to the Capitol last week. The road rage of rush hour evaporated like a morning dew. Instead, flags flew from car phone antennas and drivers waved and gave a thumbs-up when you signaled to change lanes.

You could feel it at the Capitol. Congress passed a $40 billion emergency aid bill by an unprecedented unanimous vote. But that was only part of it. When Senate Republican leader Trent Lott and his Democratic counterpart, Tom Daschle, approached the microphones this time, Lott had his arm around and his hand on the shoulder of his old political foe.

Someone said that America changed forever last week, but that is not quite right, because I am old enough to remember an America that used to be this way.

That is the easy part for us to forget, because we got off track in the sixties. A great cynicism gripped the country after the death of John Kennedy, and as we became bogged down in Vietnam, a war we never understood. We lost faith in government, our institutions and each other.

On Tuesday we somehow remembered how it used to be, and how we used to understand that we were all in this together, that any one of us could have been on one of those planes, that our children or brothers or sisters could have been in one of those buildings and that it could happen again.

Many things happened on Tuesday, and I think one of them may be that we have finally gotten past Vietnam. Those who wanted to get America's attention got it, and they will rue the day they did.

—*September 16, 2001*

Aftermath

O nly now are we coming to understand all of the ways this has affected us. Only now have the survivors realized the deep psychological impact it is having on them. Young people return to their offices and cry. Work no longer seems important. Parents worry their children will not know the kind of world they have known. We give thanks that we were not at Ground Zero when it happened, then we feel guilty and tell ourselves we didn't mean that we were glad someone else was there instead of us, and then we don't know what we mean.

I spend most of my working days on Capitol Hill. If the plane that went down in Pennsylvania was headed to the Capitol, as many now believe, perhaps I owe my life to the brave passengers who forced it to crash.

The questions we ask at times like these are those that have been asked from the beginning of time: Where does evil come from? Why do some live and others die?

We can never know. What we do recognize is that grief is a part of healing.

Yet we must not succumb to despair, nor is there reason to.

When we saw Congress cheering the president, it reflected an America united, something we have not seen in a long time, something younger generations have never seen.

American resolve is still the most powerful force on Earth. In no way does it diminish the horror we have just experienced to say that those of us of a certain age saw an America united rid the world of a far greater and more dastardly evil.

This is different, but it is doable.

Together, we can find a way to do it.

—September 23, 2001

The Origins of Hatred

When we hear the president talk about the long battle ahead, I wonder if we really understand how long and how complicated this is going to be.

Yes, we must track down Osama bin Laden and his henchmen of hate, just as we destroyed Hitler and his gang. And we will. But that is just the first part. The real enemy is not Osama; it is the ignorance that breeds the hatred that fuels his cause. This is what we have to change.

I realized what an enormous job that was going to be the other day when I heard a young Pakistani student tell an interviewer that everyone in his school knew that Israel was behind the attacks on the Twin Towers and everyone in his school knew all the Jews who worked there had stayed home that day.

What we have all come to realize now is that a large part of the world not only misunderstands us, but is teaching its children to hate us. We won't change that through short-term propaganda and spin. We must take a longer view—financially, philosophically and relentlessly.

We must help, encourage, force, if necessary, those who control that part of the world to open up, to educate their people and let them connect with the rest of the world, to let them see through an independent press and television what it is like on the other side of the tracks.

Impossible?

No. We did it in Japan and Europe in a far more difficult time after World War II. And, yes, it will be expensive, and, yes, it will take years. But it is in our own self-interest to do it.

Barricades and weapons can make us safer, but only when we conquer the poverty and ignorance that breed hatred can we be truly secure.

—December 2, 2001

Proud to Be Americans

W e are coming to the end of a year that none of us who lived through it will ever forget. Not since the assassination of John Kennedy had so many of us sat transfixed in shock before our televisions. Yet not since World War II had the nation come together as it did in those days after the attacks on the Twin Towers and the Pentagon.

I'm not one of those who believe that such things happen to make us stronger and better. I don't know why they happen. But it is during such times that we see just how strong and good we can be.

And we have seen that over and over, not just from the firemen and the policemen and the rescue workers and our brave young military people still willing to risk their lives for the rest of us, but in so many other ways as well: in the return of civility. Road rage is down, and we seem to be speaking to one another again on the streets. "How are you today?" It made us feel good just to say it.

It was a year we remembered the government wasn't the enemy, as some had been trying to tell us. We realized the government was just us, working together to do what we couldn't do alone. We realized we do need each other.

Yes, it was a year when the sorrow and anger and anxiety seemed almost unbearable. But it was also a year that made us proud to be Americans.

—*December 30, 2001*

Daily Reminders

From my perch outside the Capitol, I had a fine view of the president driving up Pennsylvania Avenue to address Congress the other night, and what a sight it was. All streets within two blocks of the Capitol had been closed, helicopters overhead, a thirty-eight-car motorcade and eighteen motorcycles, all of them roaring on to the heavily barricaded Capitol, which is now guarded by police and National Guard troops.

Is the heavy security necessary? Only a fool would say no, but it made me feel old and it made me mad because what I was seeing was so different from the Washington I saw when I came here in 1969, so different that it was like being in another country. Back then, people came and went as they pleased. Tourists strolled through our national buildings and monuments at will. Now there is so much security, they can't get close most of the time.

When I covered the Pentagon back in the 1970s, I didn't even need a press pass to get in. All of that changed in the eighties when terrorists bombed our Marine barracks in Lebanon. The barricades went up, and every year since, the security has become more oppressive and more necessary.

And that's what grates on me. When we can't walk freely through the buildings and monuments that are the symbols of our freedom, we're paying a higher price to terrorists than we may even have realized, and it didn't start on 9/11.

I hate those barricades and what they have done to the most beautiful capital city in the world, but for me, they are the daily reminders that this war has been coming for a long time and why it must be won no matter how much longer it takes.

—*February 3, 2002*

We all took pride in how America reacted
to the unprovoked attack on 9/11, but a hurricane
called Katrina caused us to question
government at every level.

Government Failed
the People

We have come through what may have been one of the worst weeks in America's history, a week in which government at every level failed the people it was created to serve.

There is no purpose for government except to improve the lives of its citizens. Yet as scenes of horror that seemed to be coming from some Third World country flashed before us, official Washington was like a dog watching television. It saw the lights and images, but did not seem to comprehend their meaning or see any link to reality.

As the floodwaters rose, local officials in New Orleans ordered the city evacuated. They might as well have told their citizens to fly to the moon. How do you evacuate when you don't have a car? No hint of intelligent design in any of this. This was just survival of the richest. By midweek a parade of Washington officials rushed before the cameras to urge patience. What good is patience to a mother who can't find food and water for a dehydrated child?

Washington was coming out of an August vacation stupor and seemed unable to refocus on business or even think straight. Why else would Speaker of the House Dennis Hastert question aloud whether New Orleans should even be rebuilt? And when he was unable to get to Washington in time to vote on emergency aid funds, Hastert had an excuse only Washington could understand: he had to attend a fund-raiser back home.

Since 9/11, Washington has spent years and untold billions reorganizing the government to deal with crises brought on by possible terrorist attacks.

If this is the result, we had better start over.

—September 4, 2005

9/11 and Hurricane Katrina

In the midst of the disaster along the coast, let us pause now to remember what happened four years ago today when we were blindsided by a heartless enemy. We were attacked that day by terrorists willing to take the lives of innocent people to advance their cause, but that day we also saw what sets us apart from such an enemy. We saw Americans who were willing to risk and, in many cases, give their lives to save the innocent.

That is the part that we must tell our children, because that is who we are and what we want them to be.

The brave firemen and policemen of New York, the passengers who gave their lives to force down hijacked Flight 93 before it could be crashed into the U.S. Capitol, and so many others showed us that day what true heroism is. Led by a decisive mayor, New York rescue teams saved countless lives as the untested young president found just the right words to rally the nation.

This time it did not happen that way.

Local officials all but panicked.

Officials at the highest level were tongue-tied, full of excuses but unable to find the words to give the nation comfort or confidence.

But as the government fumbled, the American people did not. Charities appeared from nowhere. People opened their hearts, homes, their schools. "Bring them on," went out the cry from Texas to Utah.

No, these poor people in shelters are not better off than they were back home, but they will live to see a better day.

The government dropped the ball last week, but the good and great American people picked it up, as they always do, thank God.

—*September 12, 2005*

It seemed like the usual press conference accolade when
the president turned to his emergency management chief
Michael D. Brown and told him, "Brownie, you're doing
a heck of a job!" but when FEMA's fumbling became
known, the phrase became one of derision.

A Nation's Concept
of Itself

When President Thomas Jefferson called in Lewis and Clark,
he gave them a tall order: "Find out if there is a water route
to the Pacific." Well, two hundred years ago tomorrow, finally in
sight of the Pacific Ocean, they had the answer: there was no direct
route, but they found out so much along the way that, as the *Washington Post* put it yesterday, "They recast the nation's whole concept
of itself."

Last month, President Bush gave the head of FEMA, Michael
Brown, a tall order: Get help to victims of Katrina. Brown had a
somewhat different response. As we now know from his e-mails, he
was worried about how he looked on TV. To appear hardworking, a
staffer messaged him, "Roll up your sleeves." Looking worn out was
never really a problem for Lewis and Clark.

By now, old Brownie is an easy target, but he is one more example of how government all too often worries more about how things
look and who gets credit than what's being done.

When I came to Washington thirty-eight years ago, many congressmen didn't even have press secretaries. Now spokespersons, media coaches and consultants with talking points have caused a traffic jam in government corridors.

A nation that became a nation by showing others how to do it has somehow produced a government that seems more interested in how to say it.

And one other thing: that person who told Brownie to roll up his sleeves is still on the government payroll. So is Brownie. He's one of those consultants now.

—November 7, 2005

Flood-Level Hypocrisy

I don't know about you, but I know all I need to know about the government bumbling after Hurricane Katrina.

When I tuned in to those Senate hearings Friday, I realized it is now the hypocrisy that's at flood level. And the wind speed? Forget it.

There was Old Brownie, the former FEMA chief who became the face of government ineptitude.

Now he tells us it was everyone else's fault. He says he called the White House early to warn it was bad and talked to the president.

Well, check that. He's not really sure the president was on the line.

Give me a break. You call the White House and you're not quite sure you're talking to the president?

Then there are the Democrats. They blistered Old Brownie when the levees broke, especially after the president said he was doing a heck of a job.

But now that Old Brownie is blaming higher-ups, Democrats are portraying him as some kind of victim. Give me another break. I was beginning to believe one of the Democrats might hug Old Brownie Friday.

Here's all we need to know: Old Brownie may or may not be, well, limited. But here's the larger point. By now we know this was a failure of government at every level and that the Department of Homeland Security is a monumental flop, a bureaucracy so huge it is unable to move in spite of itself.

FEMA, the disaster relief agency that Brownie ran, should be removed from Homeland Security, and its chief should report directly to the White House.

And God help us if there *is* a terrorist attack.

—February 12, 2006

Feeling Abandoned in New Orleans

I'm glad Washington got to see those tapes of government video conferences that showed government officials from the top down were warned that Hurricane Katrina held the potential for catastrophe yet did nothing but watch it happen.

But didn't we know that already? That the huge bureaucracy cobbled together after 9/11 was a monumental flop? That political hacks performed like political hacks? Yes, it was a disgrace, but after two days in New Orleans I'm convinced we have to stop the tape and go live.

The people of New Orleans I talked to feel abandoned by government at every level and forgotten by the rest of the country. But their worry is *now*. What happens next? Are the levees really going to hold next time? Will they ever collect on their flood insurance? Will they ever get their schools open again? Only twenty of more than 120 are open.

As government bureaucracies and Congress wrangle over who's to blame, there is still no real plan about what to do. What we do know is the next hurricane season is less than three months away. Sheriff Jack Stevens of nearby St. Bernard Parish, whose entire 140-person force is living in trailers, told me the other night, "No one knows what will happen if we get another big one. We're hanging on by our fingernails."

Can't we keep the tape recorder off long enough to think about that?

—*March 5, 2006*

By 2007, we thought we had heard the last of the outrages from FEMA, but we were wrong.

At FEMA, Your IQ Must Be Below This Line

The last time I was at Disney World, they had sticks of a certain height stuck in the ground with signs that said something like: "You must be this tall to ride this ride." FEMA, the disaster relief agency, must use a variation of that to hire its public relations staff.

Somewhere on their employment application form, there must be a clause that says, "Your IQ must be *below* a certain level to work here."

How else to explain FEMA's action last week when it staged a phony news conference where its employees posed as reporters and threw softball questions to agency leaders so they could tell us what a good job they were doing at the California fires?

Mind you, this is the same FEMA once headed by Michael Brown—he of "Brownie, you're doing a heckuva job" fame—that fell on its face during Katrina. While New Orleans drowned, Brownie's PR people busied themselves by e-mailing Brownie to roll up his sleeves before TV interviews so it would look like he was working hard.

Department of Homeland Security Chief Michael Chertoff said he found the phony news conference offensive, and, since it is an emergency relief outfit, I have some emergency suggestions for him.

Fire these people and the people who hired them and then explain to the new people that the best way for a disaster relief agency to get good publicity is to do a good job helping disaster victims.

As part of a massive new PR campaign, you might even consider taking the PR staff from behind their desks and sending them to deliver food and water to the fire victims.

Now that would make a great story.

—October 28, 2007

Our Finest Hour

I can't even remember where it was, but in the months after 9/11, I was giving a lecture when a young person rose with a question.

He said, "You keep talking about the brave Americans but aren't the people who flew those airplanes into the Twin Towers heroes, too? After all, they believed so deeply in their cause, they were willing to give their lives for it."

I was stunned.

"No," I told him, "those people are not heroes, nor can they ever be. They deliberately took the lives of innocent men, women and children to promote their cause. No cause, even a noble cause, is worth that.

"Americans did the opposite, over and over," I said. "They risked their lives—some gave their lives—for no reason or reward except to save the innocent." And not just at Ground Zero and the Pentagon, but all over America, people went back to work, opened their homes to those without homes, Congress passed emergency legislation, partisan differences faded, road rage vanished as the country came together as it had not come together since World War II.

Sadly, much of that feeling has drifted away, but I like to believe that deep down it is still there in all of us. We must never forget the dark day that was 9/11, but we must always remember it led to America's finest hour.

We were all heroes that day. We had to be.

—September 10, 2006

XII

HEROES

M odern communications technology has done more than make it possible to move mountains of information around the globe in an instant. It has also redefined what we mean by privacy and blurred the line between celebrity and heroism.

The new technology has made it possible for some to become famous for being famous, and because it is now possible for the rest of us to have our own websites, many are willing to share their innermost secrets in the hope of becoming celebrities.

We rail against government intrusion into our lives in the name of national security. Yet tiny self-installed cameras can be found in many college dorm rooms and the basements of private homes, placed there by those who want the rest of us to know whatever happens there. Bloggers churn out endless accounts of their frustrations, opinions and even their sex lives. The new openness has led us to add another acronym to the American vocabulary, "TMI," which stands for too much information (exclamation point optional). But the popularity of such Web outlets as YouTube and MySpace suggests that some of us who question all this may have simply arrived at a place we never thought we would reach: Old Fogy Land.

Whatever, as Paris Hilton might say, cable television with its insatiable craving for information to fill the screen between natural disasters and other significant events hasn't helped.

For me, the Too Much Information Trophy was retired the day one of the cables reported that "the embalming process had begun" on Anna Nicole Smith.

In that instance you could at least make the case that the Anna Nicole Smith story was legitimate news of a kind—it did involve millions of dollars, the life of a child and eventually a death.

But what did Paris Hilton ever do that mattered? Yet she became not only famous for being famous, her celebrity reached such a level that others who had products to sell or just wanted to focus attention on themselves would pay her to appear at their social gatherings. Sadly, such people have become trendsetters, role models—heroes and heroines—for too many young Americans. They are not heroes, they are celebrities, and there is little if any connection between the two.

Assembling the essays in this chapter reminded me again just how wide those differences usually are.

Many true heroes have become well known for what they did, but many times what they did was unpopular at the time. Nor does fame come to every hero. Parents little known outside their families may become heroes to their children, and that kind of heroism is no small thing. Some role models never know the impact they have had on those whose lives their words or actions have touched. Some heroes accomplish great things we all come to know about; others do such things as adopting handicapped children, which few know about. On 9/11, firemen and policemen put their lives at risk to save the innocent after an attack by those who killed the innocent to make their misguided point.

The lines between celebrity and heroes have blurred, but we should not forget that America came to be because of real heroes, those who had the courage to strike out into the unknown to make a better life for their children. We should remember as well that such people still walk among us, sometimes silently, sometimes not.

FDR

———

This was the week that Washington remembered Franklin Roosevelt.

His new memorial officially opened, and it is in the neighborhood where most Americans would say it ought to be, not far from the memorials of Washington and Lincoln and Jefferson, on the banks of the Potomac.

It is huge, nearly seven acres, because he was a giant, and along the way, carved into the hard granite, are the words that rallied and sustained a nation through Depression and war, and in the end, defined Roosevelt's greatness. "I hate war. The test of our progress is not whether we add to those who have much; it is whether we provide enough for those who have too little. Demoralization caused by unemployment is our greatest extravagance. We must remember that any oppression, any injustice, any hatred is a wedge designed to attack our civilization. I never forget I live in a house owned by the American people, and I have been given their trust."

In a time when we often find so little to admire in politics, it's easy to forget that for all his vision, Roosevelt was also a master politician who not only saw the way, but could somehow find a way to get there.

The historian Doris Kearns Goodwin said this week that "Even though Roosevelt did not have the benefit of public opinion polls as politicians do today, he always seemed to know where the people were at any given moment on any given issue." But, she said, "Instead of just freezing himself there like politicians do today, he felt a responsibility to move the people forward, and somehow knew exactly how and at what speed to do that. That was the difference."

—*May 4, 1997*

Eugene Lang

I t was sixteen years ago that a man named Eugene Lang was invited to talk to a group of sixth-grade students in a school in a poor neighborhood of New York's Harlem.

As the saying goes, he got a little carried away.

He was so impressed by the kids that in the middle of the talk a thought came to him, and he heard himself making them an astonishing promise. "If you will study and finish school," he told the students, "I will personally pay for your college educations." And he did.

Well, out of that idea, a foundation called I Have A Dream was formed. You don't hear much about it. The group spends its money on kids rather than self-promotion.

But Eugene Lang's original idea has led to 170 similar projects around the country, including several here in Washington. Groups adopt a class of students, mentor them and provide whatever support they need to get through elementary and high school, and then the group puts them through college or vocational school. At last count, 16,000 students were sponsored; 2,500 had gone on to college.

Today in Harlem, Eugene Lang is holding a Sweet 16 reunion for his original class. Several who were away on business trips or cramming for graduate and law school finals couldn't make it, but it will still be a bigger turnout than even Lang expected, because twenty-nine of the original class will be there, along with thirty-five of their children.

Sometimes getting a little carried away turns out just fine.

—*May 18, 1997*

John Glenn

There's been a lot of carping about whether seventy-seven-year-old John Glenn ought to be going up in space this week. You've heard the jokes about how he'll be the first astronaut allowed to pre-board and so on.

Well, a lot of it is coming from some of the younger astronauts, who, frankly, sound a little jealous when they say, "It's just a publicity stunt."

My question is: So what?

It's costing no more to send Glenn up than one of the younger pups, and for my money, if he wants to go, he deserves it.

I remember his first flight, how he showed us the "right stuff" during the depths of the Cold War. America was pretty nervous then because the Russians had caught up with us in nuclear weapons and had just beaten us into space. But Glenn risked his life and we all got our confidence back.

I also remember how mystified he was that he never got to go up again, only to later learn that President Kennedy had secretly grounded him. Some said that was because Glenn was becoming so popular, the Kennedys were afraid he might run against one of them.

So buckle up and have a good trip, John Glenn, a man who's

about the Pope's age, who has kept himself in astronaut-trim shape all these years, inspires all of us to keep pounding the old treadmill.

Besides, when you're my age, it's just nice to have an older person to look up to.

—*October 25, 1998*

Hamilton Jordan

————

Hamilton Jordan came through Washington last week. You may remember him as the boy wonder of American politics, who devised the plan an obscure governor named Jimmy Carter used to become president.

As Carter's chief of staff, Jordan became one of the most powerful men in government, and left Washington believing what he did here would be the defining experience of his life.

Today, he would tell you all of that was mostly irrelevant because he contracted cancer, and then he beat it three times. Cancer became the defining experience of his life.

These days, he and his wife run a camp for children with cancer, and he travels the country telling people to get regular checkups, to watch for cancer signs.

His message is a simple one: if cancer is found, take control of the treatment of your disease. Learn all you can about it before you commit to any treatment. He also brought some sobering statistics. Forty percent of us, he told us, will eventually get the disease. Yet we spent less on cancer last year than we will spend on our newest aircraft carrier. It is a vital message. And with his contacts, he can get it to the right places to get something done.

But as I was listening to him, I was struck by something else, as well. We can never know what's next in life, nor can we pick its defining moments. That is done for us. It's how we deal with the unexpected, the things we cannot control, that defines our life and reveals our character.

Life dealt Ham Jordan some bad cards for a while there. But the way he played them is making the world a better place, and tells us who he really is. We can all be grateful for that.

—*July 22, 2001*

Bill Proxmire

When the announcement came last week that former Wisconsin Senator William Proxmire had died at the age of ninety, I thought of the old days and what the Senate used to be—a place of giants, like Lyndon Johnson, Everett Dirksen, Hubert Humphrey, Robert Taft.

Even the demagogues like Joe McCarthy were somehow larger than life. And, oh, what characters they were!

Not so in today's money-driven politics. Yesterday's giants have been replaced mostly by good but smaller men. On the one hand, there are those who have made a science of nonstop fund-raising. On the other, there are the rich people who have tired of giving to charity and have decided instead to give themselves—a pity, really, their money did so much good.

Of all the characters who strode the Senate floor, William Proxmire was the oddest one I ever knew. Long before jogging was in vogue, he ran to work, ten miles every day. He was a vain fellow, among the first to get a face-lift and hair transplants, but he never hid it, just showed up for work, plugs in full view.

Even odder, he thought taxpayers sent him to Washington to stop spending on stupid stuff, and he saved us a bundle in his relentless quest to track down waste.

And then there was that other quirk. He refused to accept campaign contributions. Let me repeat: he refused to accept campaign contributions. And in thirty-two years in the Senate, he never spent more than two hundred dollars on a campaign, and most of that went to buy stamps to return contributions people had sent him.

I know, I know. Yesterday always looks better than it probably was. But I believe politics was a lot better when we had more characters like Bill Proxmire.

—December 18, 2005

Martin Luther King Jr.

M onday is the day we celebrate Martin Luther King Jr.'s birthday, and it got me thinking of just how much this country has changed because of him.

When I graduated from college, no black person had ever gone to any school that I had attended.

And I still remember the first black person I shook hands with. I was grown and I was in the Air Force. It wasn't because I tried to avoid it, but the opportunity had never arisen. We lived on one side of town. The black people lived on the other.

Yet in less than my lifetime—a lot less, I hope—we have gone from a country that officially sanctioned segregation to one in which it is universally condemned. The courts changed the law, but it was Martin Luther King Jr. who made us face up to the law and told us why we should obey it. And when he did, attitudes began to change.

Back in 1960, John Kennedy had to make a long speech to assure voters he could be trusted even though he was a Catholic. Think of the selling job he would have confronted had he been black back then.

Yet what struck me, when Colin Powell was thinking of running for president several years ago, was that race was the one question that never really came up.

And today, George Bush's ethnicity—read that, Texan—draws more comment than that of his secretary of state, which is hardly ever noticed. That is a big deal, and much of the credit goes to King.

In leading black people to their rightful place, he led all of us to a better world. Tomorrow is a day off for most of us. Use part of it to tell the kids what Martin Luther King Jr. did, not just for African-Americans but for all of us.

—January 20, 2002

AFTERWORD

No one has to remind me I've been around awhile—my body tells me every time I climb a flight of stairs or squint when I come to the fine print or sit down to a meal and have to pass on the carbs and the dessert—but one day during the summer of 2007, it hit me just how long I've been a reporter.

I was telling someone about how I got my first job, about that day when I walked into a little radio station in Fort Worth, Texas, told the news director I could type and convinced him to take me on as a reporter for the princely sum of one dollar an hour. Then it dawned on me. That had all taken place in the summer of 1957, fifty years ago. By the end of that day, I had taught myself to type, and from that day forward for more than half a century, I have received a weekly paycheck for reporting the news.

I was a college sophomore when I applied for that job, and I worked forty-four hours a week covering the police beat for the station until graduation; then came three years in the Air Force, where I edited a series of military publications. After the service, I returned to Fort Worth and the police beat. Within months, I changed desks at the police press room and began covering the cops for the *Fort Worth Star-Telegram*. An assignment as the newspaper's first correspondent in Vietnam led to a job at the local television station, and that in turn led to Washington and CBS News, where, in 1969, I joined the network's legendary Washington bureau. I never left. In the ensuing years, I would report from all over the world. In 1979 and 1980, I anchored the network's *Morning News* from New York, an assignment that was a monumental flop, and in 2005, I commuted to New York to anchor the *Evening News* for a year and a half, an assignment that proved more successful, but always the Washington bureau was my home base.

In his charming book about the bureau during its glory days of the 1960s and early 1970s, Roger Mudd called it *The Place to Be*. For me, it was the only place I ever wanted to be.

Once my arm gave out and it became clear I would never be a ballplayer, I had only one goal—to be a reporter. When I reported for work in Washington that first day in 1969, I was not only living the dream that had been with me for as long as I could remember, I was becoming a colleague of those who had been my heroes—Eric Sevareid, Dan Rather, Roger Mudd, Marvin Kalb, Daniel Schorr and George Herman. On that first day, I was like a Little Leaguer who had been called off the bench to pinch-hit at Yankee Stadium. I never got over the thrill of working for my boyhood idol, Walter Cronkite, and being part of his great Washington team. I loved it then and I have loved every minute since.

These days, my office is the same one where Eric Sevareid once sat, and I suppose it is testament to my longevity that when I was given the space, I was the only one who realized it had once been Eric's. All the people who worked in the bureau when I came to CBS have moved on. Some moved to other places for CBS, some left for what they believed were better jobs, others left in bitterness, some retired, and a fair number died.

Over the years, I would cover all the big Washington beats—the Pentagon, the White House, the State Department and Congress— and I reported from all over the world. It is fair to say in retrospect, I rose rapidly. Within a year of joining CBS, I became a correspondent and was assigned one of the most important beats. But there were disappointments along the way. When I moved the family to New York for the *Morning News* assignment, I was told that it might put me in the running to replace Walter when he retired in 1980. I would later learn that I had never seriously been considered, and when the job went to Dan Rather, Roger Mudd resigned. I just asked to return to Washington and started over, the best decision I ever made. For me, when one door closed, I looked for other doors, and somehow, something else always came along.

It was Washington and my fascination with how government worked that always saved me. By 1989, I was ensconced on Capitol Hill, covering what I loved best, politics and politicians.

When I was asked to anchor the *Evening News* in 2005, no one was more surprised than I. When Dan got the job in 1980, I had concluded that was that. We were close enough in age that I figured by the time he retired, I would be too old to be considered a replacement, so I never thought about it again.

Once I had the job in 2005 (albeit temporarily, while the search was on for a permanent replacement), I found it interesting and a great unexpected adventure, but I also realized that had I gotten it back in 1980, my life would not have been nearly as fulfilling. I never found many stories in the studio. I loved Washington and being where the news was. When I wrote *This Just In* in 2003, someone said it was one of the few books written by someone in television who wasn't trying to get even with someone. The remark was accurate, I have no complaints. If my life ended tomorrow, I would not feel shortchanged. Few people get a chance to do as adults what they dreamed of doing as children, and I am one of the lucky few. I got a chance to see and do far more than I ever thought I would.

As I sit now in Eric Sevareid's office—and to me it will always be Eric's—I have come to the part of life where I realize that the number of years before me will be far short of the years I have already lived. John Kennedy once said no man would trade his time for that of another, and I am glad that I got to spend my time on earth during the American Century. I got to see man leave the planet for the first time; I was there when our country corrected the great wrong of segregation; I can remember those dark days when my parents' generation confronted and defeated Nazis, the greatest evil the world had ever known; and I saw the American system prevail over European socialism, communism and the thoughts of Chairman Mao. America became the greatest and most influential power the world had known since the rise of the Roman Empire, and I was there to see and experience it.

I am no longer as certain of as many things as I once was, the certainties of youth give way to hard lessons of experience, but I have come to believe I know a little more about some things than I once did.

Over and over in my own life, I have come to understand that what seemed the worst experiences at the time produced the best lessons. Most of the time, I just learned that patience was usually the best course. If something didn't work out for me at the moment, in time something else would come along. It was always hard to wait, but for me usually worth it.

I also learned that the small things in life would often produce the most treasured memories. Certainly it was no big feat for a professional climber, but when my wife and I were offered the chance in the summer of 2007 to scale Mt. Rushmore and sit on George Washington's head, the climb became a metaphor for our marriage of four decades. We had no idea what we were getting into at the start, probably wouldn't have tried it had we known how strenuous it would be, took a detour or two along the way, but in the end we made it. The memory of that day and others like it will be with us forever, more precious than any gift or accolade.

As for politics and government, I would best describe myself as still looking for final answers, but here are some of the things I have come to believe.

DEMOCRACY MUST COME FROM WITHIN; IT CANNOT BE IMPOSED FROM WITHOUT.

If we have learned one lesson from Vietnam and Iraq, that should be it. In Vietnam we wandered into the end of a colonial war, believing our national interest required us to draw a line and tell the Communists they could not cross it. In exchange for drawing that line in their country, we offered the gift of Jeffersonian democracy to people who had been ruled for thousands of years by outsiders, people who knew little of the world beyond their own villages, and who believed power accrued to whoever had the guns and continued only as long as the ammunition lasted. Why shouldn't they have believed that? It was the only thing they had ever known. We went to Vietnam wanting neither land nor treasure but we never understood why the Vietnamese failed to recognize that we were somehow different from all the other foreigners who had come there before us.

In Iraq, the power vacuum we created unleashed forces that had only one thing in common—a blood hatred for each other that had been smoldering for thousands of years. To believe as we did that driving Saddam from power would somehow cause such forces to forget past differences, adopt Western-style government about which they knew nothing, and share power was not only unrealistic but, in retrospect, ludicrous.

We may have refined democracy in America, but we didn't invent it, nor was our unique system of checks and balances something that just came to the founders in the night and they decided to give it a try. Their thinking was informed by hundreds of years of debating and reasoning and dealing with people's rights—a debate that had begun with the Magna Carta in the thirteenth century. Democracy may be the best of all forms of government, but one size does not fit all, and understanding what it is and how it works takes some time.

AMERICA MAY BE THE WORLD'S MOST POWERFUL NATION, BUT IT DOES BEST WHEN IT WORKS WITH OTHERS.

From the Marshall Plan and the rebuilding of Europe to the United Nations and on to the first Gulf War and the coalition of countries brought together by President George H. W. Bush, modern America working in concert with its allies is a wonder to behold. Yet time after time, when we have tried to go it alone, our reach exceeded our grasp. I have always felt that one of the tragedies of the Iraq war was that some American leaders in their heart of hearts really preferred to go it alone. They were determined to show the world that we could do it, and that it would be a lesson to the world that would somehow enhance our security and place among nations. I can remember officials telling me that America's military was so powerful it really needed no help and that in fact, adding foreign forces just slowed the operation down. They may have been right, but when we left the impression that we needed no help and wanted no advice, our wishes were granted. We got no help and, rather than advice, blistering criticism when things went wrong, which is usually the case when others have no investment in the undertaking and no stake in the outcome.

AMERICA LEADS BEST AND HAS THE MOST INFLUENCE WHEN IT LEADS BY EXAMPLE.

Hubert Humphrey once said the 1964 Civil Rights Act was our most effective foreign policy initiative—not because it had anything to do with foreign policy, but because it showed the world what kind of people we were and that our system of government worked.

OUR REAL STRENGTH IS NOT OUR WEAPONS, BUT OUR CORE VALUES AND THE WAY OF LIFE THEY MAKE POSSIBLE.

During the Cold War, we built the greatest arsenal of weapons known to man, and those weapons kept the Soviet Union at bay but they did not win the war. The war was won when the peoples of Eastern Europe looked across the Iron Curtain and saw that the people on the other side had a better way of life and they wanted some of it. They didn't want rockets and bombs, they wanted washing machines and television sets and schools and a say in how their communities were being run. When they realized their system of government couldn't provide that kind of life, the walls came down and the Communist order collapsed. What the Communists misunderstood was that in the television age, secrets could no longer be kept on the other side of the tracks.

When the Berlin Wall came down, German young people sang "We Shall Overcome," the anthem of our own civil rights movement. Could there be a better reason for pride in our system or a greater validation of our own values than that?

DEMOCRACIES SHOULD ENGAGE IN NO WARS UNLESS THE SACRIFICE IS EQUALLY SHARED.

We have the finest army in the world, but the sacrifices of war are being borne by one half of one percent of us—our all-volunteer force and their families. The lives of the rest of us are largely unaffected by the war, our taxes were not raised, food is plentiful and luxury items abound for those who can afford them. If we did not read the newspapers or watch television, most of us could go through the day unaware that a war was going on. To me, this does not seem right or, in the long run, healthy for a nation created upon the principle that the responsibilities and benefits of citizenship are shared equally by every person. I remember the days of my childhood when World War II touched every family. Today, some Americans do not even know a person connected to the military.

WHEN WE ADOPT THE METHODS OF THOSE WHO HATE US, WE WEAKEN OUR SECURITY.

We must practice what we preach. We don't need secret prisons, and torture must never be part of our national policy. Those are the tactics of those who oppose us and that is what we must make sure the rest of the world understands. More important, we must be certain our children understand that.

I HAVE LIVED long enough and seen enough to retain confidence in America and the good judgment of her people, but I have also learned that nothing is forever.

Will Durant is my favorite historian, and he once wrote that while Rome was not built in a day, neither did it fall overnight. He reminds us that the fall of the Roman Empire actually took place over the span of three hundred years, longer than any democracy has existed. In history's long view, the idea of democracy is fairly new. It can survive only so long as its citizens are willing to nurture and defend it. For me, that is the great lesson to be passed on to those who come after us.

As wondrous as it is, we must never take America for granted.

ACKNOWLEDGMENTS

This book happened because Neil Nyren, the publisher and editor in chief at Putnam, thought it was time for a collection of commentaries, and any excuse to work with Neil is good enough for me, so I got right on it. Neil edited my memoir *This Just In*, which came out in 2003, and unlike many editing experiences I have heard about, working with Neil couldn't have been more enjoyable. Neil is that rare bird in the editors' aviary. He lets authors write their own books. When I circulated my memoir proposal to several publishers, more than one editor said, "No, what you really want to do is this." No, what I really wanted to do was what I had proposed, and I told one, "You have a great idea for a book; you should write it. That's not what I want to write." Neil lets you write your book and, with a quick edit here and a suggestion there, he makes it better. Thanks, Neil.

I must also thank my boss Sean McManus, the president of CBS News, for clearing the bureaucratic underbrush and getting the permissions necessary to publish the commentaries. Sean has been a great boss and I treasure his friendship.

Thanks also to super-agent Esther Newberg. Whether it is a barroom argument or a literary negotiation, I always want Esther on my side of the table. Thanks also to Carin Pratt, executive producer, and producers Denise Li and Arlene Weisskopf. The four of us make up the entire editorial staff of *Face the Nation*, and since March 1991 we have managed to get the broadcast on the air on time every Sunday and off the air before time ran out. My friend Jan

Crawford Greenburg still finds time in her busy life to give me wise counsel and advice, and for nearly twenty years *Evening News* producer Mary Hager has been there to help me meet a thousand deadlines. I also wish to thank three extraordinary women who served as my research assistants in recent years: Jan Mann, who kept me in the right city at the right time when I was anchoring *Face the Nation* from Washington and commuting to New York to anchor the *CBS Evening News*; Michelle Levi, the young dynamo who took over for Jan when I returned to Washington; and Kaylee Hartung, who stepped in when Michelle was promoted to our political campaign unit and never missed a beat—either during the day or at night when she took the occasional turn as a backup singer in my country-western band Honky Tonk Confidential. Mary, Jan, Michelle and Kaylee are more than colleagues, they're part of the family.

And speaking of family, there's no one quite like my wife, Pat, who has always been there when I needed her and no more so than on those Saturday nights when the well had run dry and I had nothing to offer as commentary for Sunday's broadcast. On more than one late Saturday night, she has said, "Well, you've been ranting all week about such and such, write about that!" and usually I did. She can still untangle my thoughts when I need it and, after more than forty years of marriage, still laughs at my jokes. That's hard to beat.

—*Bob Schieffer, Washington, D.C.*